BERLIN

ZWISCHEN GESCHICHTE UND ZUKUNFT

ENTRE HISTORIA Y FUTURO

BETWEEN HISTORY AND THE FUTURE

JOVIS

Unser Dank gilt allen beteiligten Architekten, Autoren und Fotografen sowie Institutionen und Firmen, die uns bei der Realisierung des Projektes unterstützt haben.

We would like to express our thanks to all the architects, authors and photographers involved, as well as the institutions and companies who supported us in the realisation of this project.

Queremos expresar nuestro agradecimiento a todos los arquitectos, autores y fotógrafos así como instituciones y empresas que junto con nosotros han hecho posible la realización de este Proyecto.

Bildnachweis / Index of Illustrations / Índice de Ilustraciones

Der Verlag hat sich bemüht, alle Rechteinhaber zu ermitteln. Bitte wenden Sie sich bei berechtigten Ansprüchen an den Verlag, damit Fehler oder Auslassungen korrigiert werden können.

Every effort has been made to contact copyright holders. The publishers would be pleased to hear from copyright holders to rectify any errors or omissions.

La editorial ha procurado identificar a todos los titulares de derechos. En caso de posibles reclamaciones por favor diríjase a nosotros a fin de posiblitar la corrección de errores u omisiones.

ARGENTA Internationale Anlagegesellschaft mbH: 12 o.
Axel Schultes Architekten: 56 u.
Berliner Ensemble: *Fotografin* Monika Rittershaus 19 u.
Botanischer Garten Berlin: U6
Botschaft der Vereinigten Staaten von Mexiko: *Fotograf* Bernhard Kroll 48 u.r.
Bundesministerium der Finanzen: *Fotograf* Jürgen Flemnitz 10 u.l., 10 u.r.
Bundesministerium für Wirtschaft und Technologie: *Fotograf* Stefan Müller 42 u.
Deutsche Bahn AG: 54 o., 55 u.
Die Bevollmächtigte des Saarlandes beim Bund: *Fotograf* René Mailänder 45 o.l.
ECE Projektmanagement: *Fotograf* Michael Haddenhorst 13 o.
FALCON CREST airphotos: 41 o.
Flaskamp GmbH: *Fotograf* Tobias Kleinod 44
Friedrich, R. (*Fotograf*): 38 o.
Friedrichstadtpalast: 18 u.
Galeries Lafayette: 14 u.
gmp - von Gerkan Marg & Partner: 54 m. *Fotograf* Hans Bach
Götz Bellmann & Walter Böhm: *Fotograf* Florian Bolk 22 o.l., 22 o.m., 22 o.r.
Graetz Nöfer Tyrra, Architektengesellschaft Friedrichswerder: 27 u.l., 27 u.m., 27 u.r.
Groth Gruppe: *Fotograf* Bernhard Kroll 47 o., 47 u.l., 47 u.r., 48 o.
HVB Projekt GmbH: 37 u.l.
Haus der Kulturen der Welt: 40 o.
Hesse, Udo (*Fotograf*): 19 o.
Hilmer + Sattler + Albrecht: *Perspektivzeichnungen* Jadegan Azizi 36 o., 36 u., 37 o., 37 u.r.
Höger Hare Architekten: *Fotografin* Simone Rosenberg 20 o.l. / *Fotograf* Matthias Broneske 20 o.r.
Ingrid Hentschel/Axel Oestreich: *Fotograf* M. Schuppenhauer 54 u.
Jagdfeld FriedrichstadtPassagen Quartier 206: *Fotografen* Jörn Vanhöfen, Bernhard Schurian 15 o., 15 u.l., 15 u.r.
JOVIS Verlag: *Fotografin* Kerstin Müller 13 u., 39 u.
J.S.K Dipl. Ing. Architekten: *Fotograf* Michael Krüger 51 o.l., 51 o.r.
KNY&WEBER, 2001: 32 o.
Kisling, Annette (*Fotografin*): 9 o.l., 9 o.r.
Kujehl, Achim (*Fotograf*): 33 u.
Landesarchiv Berlin: 4
Lindner, Michael (*Fotograf*): 49 o., 49 u.
Meinel, Udo (*Fotograf*): 26 o.
Meyer, Stefan (*Fotograf*): 43 o., 43 u., 48 u.l., 53 o., 53 u.l.
Modersohn & Freiesleben: *Fotograf* Stefan Müller 35 u.
Museum für Kommunikation Berlin: *Fotograf* Schlemmer 10 o.
Müller, Stefan (*Fotograf*): 11 u.
Nalbach + Nalbach: *Fotograf* Stefan Müller 20 u.l., 20 u.r., 51 u.l. / *Fotograf* Reinhard Görner 50 u., 51 u.r.
PSP Pysall, Stahrenberg & Partner: *Fotograf* Reinhard Görner 26 u., 32 u.
Partner für Berlin/FTB-Werbefotografie:U1, U3, U4, 24, 40 u., 42 o., 46, 52, 56 o., 7 u.
Presse- und Informationsamt des Landes Berlin: *Fotograf* W. Gerling 38 u., 39 o., 53 u.l. / *Fotograf* G. Schneider U2, U8, 5, 6 u., 8 o., 8 u., 39 m. / *Fotograf* Thie U5, U7, 7 o., 7 m., 11 o., 14 o., 18 o., 22 u., 25, 33 o., 41 u., 55 m.
Profitlich, Florian (*Fotograf*): 27 o., 30-31
RKW Rhode Kellermann Wawrowsky / Architektur + Städtebau: *Perspektiven* Branca Kaminski 17 o., 17 u.
RSE Projektmanagement AG: 50 o.l., 50 o.r.
Richters, Christian (*Fotograf*): 45 o.r., 45 u.
Schippel, Alexander (*Fotograf*): 6 o., 21, 23, 28, 29, 34 o.l., 34 o.r., 34 u., 35 o., 55 o.
Spangenberg, Gerhard: 9 u.l., 9 u.r.
Thomas van den Valentyn: *Fotograf* Rainer Mader 12 u.
Züblin/Archimation: 16 o., 16 u.

Umschlag / Cover / Cubierta
Susanne Rösler

Gestaltung / Design / Diseño
Jürgen Freter

Redaktion / Editing / Redacción
Gero Drake, Ines von Ploetz, Yamin von Rauch

Lithographie / Lithography / Litografía
Satzinform, Berlin

Druck und Bindung / Printing and binding / Impresión y encuadernación
Offizin Andersen Nexö Leipzig, Zwenkau

Übersetzung ins Englische / English translation / Traducción al inglés:
Ian Cowley, Catherine Kerkhoff-Saxon
Übersetzung ins Spanische / Spanish translation / Traducción al español
SWB Communications: Gemma Correa-Buján,
La Academia: Susana Fuentes, Andreas Wuethrich

jovis Verlag GmbH
Kurfürstenstraße 15/16
10785 Berlin

ISBN 3-931321-79-7

Guido Brendgens

Ruhelose Metropole Berlin

Lässt sich eine Stadt wie Berlin überhaupt mit wenigen Worten beschreiben? Eine Metropole, die sich dem Besucher so widersprüchlich und heterogen, so unzugänglich und offen, so städtisch und dörflich zugleich präsentiert? Und die sich bei jedem seiner Besuche so sehr verändert zu haben scheint, dass er kaum noch etwas kennt und nichts mehr wieder erkennt?

Es ist, als sei der stetige Wandel ein Wesenszug der Stadt, die bis heute einen Hang zu besitzen scheint, den Zerstörungen von außen – durch Kriege – eigene hinzuzufügen, um sich dann neu zu erschaffen, ganze Quartiere aus dem Boden zu stampfen und Altes vergessen zu machen. Geschichtsbewusstsein hatte hier selten etwas mit Bewahrung von Tradition zu tun. Und so wirkt die Stadt heute wie ein Flickenteppich der Epochen, uneinheitlich, unfertig und doch immer wieder im Aufbruch begriffen.

Die Metropole begann um 1230 als Idyll, als kleinstädtische Siedlung an der Kreuzung zweier wichtiger Handelswege, angelegt an einer besonders flachen Stelle der Spree, um den fahrenden Kaufleuten die Überquerung des Flusses zu ermöglichen. 1432 schloss sich Berlin mit dem eng benachbart auf einer Spreeinsel liegenden Cölln zusammen und man errichtete ein gemeinsames Rathaus – ganz neutral auf einer Brücke. Von alldem ist heute so gut wie nichts mehr erhalten, und von den wenigen alten Gebäuden der Stadt ist so manches weit weniger historisch-original, als der Besucher vermuten würde. Das rekonstruierte Nikolaiviertel ist überwiegend nur ein nachempfundenes Alt-Berlin, entstanden in den 1980er Jahren. Selbst die Nikolaikirche, das älteste Bauwerk Berlins und ein herausragendes Beispiel märkischer Backsteingotik, ist zu großen Teilen ein Wiederaufbau.

Das Fehlen eines architektonischen Geschichtsbewusstseins tritt besonders schmerzlich am Schlossplatz zutage, einer heute öden innerstädtischen Brachfläche. Die im II. Weltkrieg stark beschädigte ehemalige Residenz der preußischen Könige und deutschen Kaiser wurde 1950 – wohl aus politischen Gründen – von der Staatsführung der DDR gesprengt. Für Berlin bedeutete das einen unwiederbringlichen Verlust, war die Stadt doch über Jahrhunderte auf diesen architektonischen Mittelpunkt hin ausgerichtet. Der geplante Wiederaufbau des Berliner Schlosses als Neubau mit rekonstruierter historischer Fassade ist heute eine der umstrittensten architektonischen Fragen in der Stadt.

Behutsamer immerhin ging man mit anderen Schlössern um, die sich die Hohenzollern in der Umgebung ihrer Residenzstadt errichten ließen. So wurde das nach Kriegseinwirkungen stark beschädigte Schloss Charlottenburg wieder aufgebaut. Johann Friedrich Eosander von Göthe war es, der der großzügig gestalteten Anlage seinerzeit ihren wirkungsvollen Kuppelturm gegeben hatte, dessen Motiv in der Berliner Architektur

Guido Brendgens

Berlin – the restless metropolis

Can a city like Berlin possibly be described in just a few words? This metropolis simultaneously presenting itself to a visitor as so contradictory and heterogeneous, so inaccessible and open, so urban and rural? Moreover, one that seems to have changed so very much with every new visit, that a person hardly knows anything anymore and hardly recognizes anything?

Continuous change seems to be a characteristic of this city. Until today it seems to have had a tendency of compounding the destruction inflicted externally by wars in order to create complete new districts out of nothing and eradicate the old. Historical awareness rarely has anything to do with protecting tradition here. This is why Berlin today seems like a patchwork of epochs, non-uniform, unfinished and yet constantly in the process of emerging.

The metropolis started around 1230 as an idyll, a provincial settlement at the crossroads of two important trade routes. It was laid out on an especially flat part of the River Spree, in order to enable travelling merchants to cross the river. In 1432, Berlin fused with Cölln, a very near neighbour on an island in the Spree. They built a new joint town hall at a neutral location on a bridge. Practically nothing of all this remains today. In fact, some of the city's few old buildings remaining are far less historically original than the visitor would presume. The reconstructed Nikolaiviertel is now primarily just a copy of Old Berlin created in the 1980s. Even the Nikolai Church, the oldest building in Berlin and an outstanding example of Northern German brick Gothic, is mostly a reconstruction.

The absence of architectonic historical awareness is especially painfully apparent at Schlossplatz. The square, which used to be at the front of the Royal Palace, is today a dreary city centre wasteland. The former residency of the Prussian Kings and German Kaisers was badly damaged in World War II but it was not pulled down until 1950. The East German government blew it up more for political reasons. It represented an irretrievable loss for Berlin, since the city had been aligned towards this architectural centre for centuries. Today, the plan to rebuild this Berlin Palace with a reconstructed historical facade is one of the most controversial architectonic questions in the city.

At least the other palaces the Hohenzollerns built near their royal seat were treated with more caution. Charlottenburg Palace was reconstructed after being badly damaged in the war. It was Johann Friedrich Eosander von Göthe who gave the generously designed facility its effective dome tower at that time. Its motif was later to be picked up repeatedly in Berlin architecture.

At one stage, the residency was extended westwards along both sides of the road Unter den Linden. With its decorative geometrical squares, Pariser Platz, Leipziger Platz and Rondell (today

Guido Brendgens

Berlín, una metrópoli sin descanso

¿Puede describirse una ciudad como Berlín, con sólo pocas palabras?, ¿una metrópoli que se presenta al visitante tan contradictoria y al mismo tiempo tan heterogénea, tan inaccesible y tan abierta, tan urbana y tan rústica?, ¿y que en cada una de sus visitas parece haber cambiado tanto que el visitante apenas si conoce algo y no reconoce casi nada?

Es como si la transformación contínua fuese un rasgo caracterísico de la ciudad que hasta hoy parece ser propensa a añadir las propias destrucciones a las provocadas desde fuera por las guerras para crearse entonces a sí misma de nuevo, erigir de la nada barrios enteros y hacer olvidar lo viejo. La conciencia histórica raramente tenía aquí algo que ver con el preservar de la tradición. Y, de esta manera, la ciudad parece hoy una alfombra de épocas remendada y no uniforme, inacabada y extendida en contínuo resurgimiento.

La metrópoli comenzó como un idílio alrededor de 1230. Se trataba de un emplazamiento provinciano en el cruce dos dos importantes vías comerciales. Estaba situado en un emplazamiento especialmente llano del Spree para hacer posible que los comerciantes de paso cruzasen el río. En 1432 Berlín se unificó con Cölln, pueblo vecino situado en una isla del Spree y fue erigido, muy neutral sobre un puente, un ayuntamiento consunto. De todo ello no queda hoy prácticamente nada y, de los pocos edificios antiguos de la ciudad, se conservan en su estado histórico original muchos menos de los que el visitante supondría. El reconstruido barrio Nikolaiviertel es, en su mayor parte, sólamente un Berlín antiguo surgido a imitación de los años 80 del siglo pasado. Incluso la iglesia Nikolaikirche, el edificio más antiguo de Berlín y ejemplo sobresaliente del Gótico de ladrillo marcado, es en gran parte una reconstrucción.

La carencia de una conciencia histórica se evidencia de un modo especialmente doloroso en la Plaza del Palacio (Schlossplatz), un terreno urbano actualmente baldío y despoblado. La antigua residencia de los reyes prusianos y emperadores alemanes, que había resultado muy dañada durante la Segunda Guerra Mundial, fue dinamitada en 1950 por razones políticas por el gobierno de la RDA. Esto supuso para Berlín una pérdida irrecuperabile pues la ciudad había estado orientada durante siglos hacia este centro arquitectónico. La proyectada reconstrucción del Palacio Berlinés como un edificio nuevo con la fachada histórica reconstruida es actualmente una de las cuestiones arquitectónicas más polémicas en la ciudad.

Con otros palacios que los Hohenzollern habían hecho erigir en los alrededores de su ciudad residencia se actuó al menos más prudentemente. Así se reconstruyó el Palacio de Charlottenburg en el tan generosamente estructurado recinto de su impresionante torre con cúpula, motivo que más tarde habría de ser retomado una y otra vez en la arquitectura de Berlín.

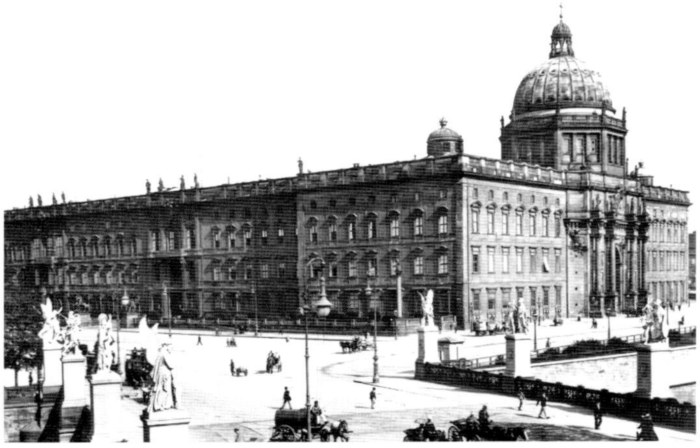

Berliner Schloss • Berlin Palace • Palacio de Berlin

später immer wieder aufgegriffen werden sollte. Die Residenzstadt wurde einst beiderseits der Straße Unter den Linden nach Westen hin erweitert. Mit ihren geometrischen Schmuckplätzen, dem Pariser und dem Leipziger Platz sowie dem Rondell (Mehringplatz) entsprach die Stadterweiterung den Idealvorstellungen barocken Städtebaus. Auch der Gendarmenmarkt wurde äußerst repräsentativ gestaltet, mit den von Karl von Gontard 1780-85 errichteten einheitlichen Turmbauten, dem Deutschen und dem Französischen Dom. Architektur war in Berlin immer auch politisches Programm: Friedrich der Große schuf mit dem Forum Fridericianum zugleich eine neue Stadtmitte neben der Staatsmitte, die sich durch die Förderung von Wissenschaft und Kunst fortschrittlich zeigen sollte.

Das 19. Jahrhundert war dann das Jahrhundert Karl Friedrich Schinkels, der in der Stadt wahre Meisterwerke klassizistischer Baukunst verwirklichte. Zahlreiche Schüler setzten sein Schaffen fort. Die architektonische Virtuosität Schinkels zeigt sich nicht zuletzt in der Unterschiedlichkeit der Bauaufgaben – von der Neuen Wache über das Schauspielhaus am Gendarmenmarkt und die Friedrichswerdersche Kirche bis zum Alten Museum.

Die Kaiserzeit, die das Stadtbild nachhaltig prägte, und vor allem die Goldenen Zwanziger, als Berlin zur modernen Weltstadt aufstieg, gelten als Glanzzeit: Berlin strahlte von Theatern, Kinos und glitzernden Revuen, besaß ein unvergleichlich reiches Kultur- und ein pulsierendes Nachtleben. Auch die Architektur dieser Jahre spiegelte die Bewegung der neuen Zeit. Sie bot mit innovativen Bauten dynamische Eck- und Platzlösungen und reagierte vielfältig auf die beständig anwachsenden Verkehrsbedürfnisse der pulsierenden Millionenstadt. An diesen in den 1920er Jahren geborenen „Mythos Berlin“ würde die Stadt seit 1990 gerne wieder anknüpfen. Doch die Zeiten haben sich verändert.

Die Umgestaltungspläne der Nationalsozialisten sahen den Abriss ganzer Stadtteile vor, der Platz schaffen sollte für eine neue, gigantische Herrschaftskulisse, eine Architektur zur Demonstration ewiger Macht. Durch die Zerstörungen des Zweiten Weltkriegs wurden diese Abrisspläne schließlich hinfällig.

Mehringplatz), this expansion of the city corresponded to the ideals of baroque urban development. The Gendarmenmarkt was also arranged in an extremely imposing manner with the German and French Domes, uniform tower buildings constructed by Karl von Gontard in 1780-85. Architecture was always a political programme as well in Berlin: Frederick the Great created his Forum Fridericianum, simultaneously creating a new city centre next to the centre of the state, one that was intended to show its progressive side by supporting science and art.

The 19th century was then the century of Karl Friedrich Schinkel, who realized true masterpieces of classical architecture in the city. Numerous pupils continued his creative work. Schinkel's architectonic virtuosity is revealed not least in the variety of the works he built – from the Neue Wache, a royal guard house, to the Theatre at the Gendarmenmarkt and from Friedrichswerder Church to the Old Museum.

The imperial era and above all the "Golden Twenties" are looked upon as Berlin's heyday. The former had a lasting impression on the townscape, and in the latter, it advanced to being a modern metropolis. Berlin now radiated with theatres, cinemas and glittering revues, had an incomparably rich cultural life and pulsating nightlife. The architecture of these years reflected the movement of the new era. It offered dynamic corner and spatial solutions with innovative buildings and reacted in a variety of ways to the continuously growing traffic needs of the pulsating big city. Ever since the city was reunified in 1990, it has dreamed of resurrecting this 1920s' myth of Berlin. Times, however, have changed.

The National Socialists' plans for redesigning the city envisaged tearing down whole districts in order to create room for a new mighty and colossal setting, for architecture intended to demonstrate eternal power. In the end, the destruction caused during the Second World War invalidated these demolition plans.

Large parts of the city had become one expanse of rubble. The situation was not exactly untimely for many town planners however – allowing them to make a clean sweep for a necessary new start. This took many forms: a greened townscape was created in the Hansaviertel in West Berlin along with the ever-present city motorway. The capital of East Germany arose in the historic centre of divided Berlin - with broad traffic axes, large spaces for parades and the Television Tower dwarfing everything else. In addition to East Berlin's mass-produced architectural articles, such as the housing estates built of pre-fabricated panels, there were also ambitious projects like Stalinallee (Karl-Marx-Allee since 1961), a main

La ciudad residencia fue ampliada antaño hacia el oeste por ambos lados de la avenida Unter den Linden. Con sus geométricas plazas decoradas – Pariser Platz, Leipziger Platz y Rondell (hoy Mehringplatz) – la ampliación de la ciudad correspondía al concepto ideal del urbanismo barroco. También la plaza Gendarmenmarkt fue configurada muy representativamente mediante los uniformes edificios con torres erigidos entre 1780 y 1785 por Karl von Gontard, la Catedral Alemana (Deutscher Dom) y la Francesa (Französicher Dom). La arquitectura en Berlín también fue siempre un programa político : Con el Forum Fridericianum Federico el Grande creó al mismo tiempo un nuevo centro urbano junto al centro del Estado el cual habría de mostrarse de un modo progresista mediante el impulso de las ciencias y la cultura.

El siglo XIX, fue el de Karl Friedrich Schinkel quien realizó en la ciudad verdaderas obras maestras de la arquitectura clasicista. Numerosos discípulos continuaron su creación. El virtuosismo arquitectónico de Schinkel se manifesta no en último término en la variedad de funciones de los edificios, desde la Neue Wache hasta el Schauspielhaus en el Gendarmenmarkt pasando por la Friedrichswerdesche Kirche hasta el Altes Museum.

La época Imperial, que marcó la imagen de la ciudad de forma duradera y, sobre todo, los dorados años veinte, cuando Berlín se convirtió en una moderna metrópoli, constituyen su época dorada: Berlín resplandecía con teatros, cines y centelleantes revistas, poseía una cultura incomparablemente rica y una animada vida nocturna. También la arquitectura de estos años reflejaba el movimiento de la nueva época. Mediante edificios innovativos ofrecía soluciones para edificar esquinas y lugares dinámicos y reaccionaba de múltiples formas frente a las necesidades de un tráfico en contínuo crecimiento en una palpitante ciudad de varios millones de habitantes. Desde 1990, a la ciudad le hubiese gustado reanudar este "mito de Berlín" nacido en los años 20 del siglo pasado. Pero los tiempos han cambiado.

Los planes de reformas de los nacionalsocialistas preveían el derribo de barrios enteros con lo que habría que crear un espacio nuevo y gigantesco escenario de dominación, una arquitectura que demostrase un poder eterno. Estos planes de derribo finalmente perdieron su validez a causa de las destrucciones de la Segunda Guerra Mundial. Amplias partes de la ciudad se habían convertido en un campo de ruinas lo que, sin embargo, no vino mal a muchos proyectistas urbanos, como si de una Tabla rasa se tratase con vistas a un necesario nuevo comienzo el cual se configuró de la ciudad. En el centro histórico del Berlín dividido surgió la capital de la RDA con amplios ejes para el tráfico, zonas de despliegue y la torre de la televisión alzándose sobre todas las cosas. Junto a los objetos arquitectónicos de masas del Berlín Oriental, como son las construcciones de bloques de pisos, hubo también proyectos ambiciosos como la avenida Stalinallee (desde 1961 Karl-Marx-Allee), una obra magistral siguiendo el

Weite Teile der Stadt waren ein Trümmerfeld geworden, was vielen Stadtplanern jedoch gar nicht ungelegen kam – als Tabula rasa für einen notwendigen Neuanfang. Dieser war vielgestaltig: So entstand in West-Berlin im Hansaviertel eine durchgrünte Stadtlandschaft, aber auch die omnipräsente Stadtautobahn. Im historischen Zentrum des geteilten Berlin entstand die Hauptstadt der DDR – mit breiten Verkehrsachsen, Aufmarschplätzen und dem alles überragenden Fernsehturm. Neben Ost-Berlins architektonischer Massenware wie den Plattenbauten gab es auch ambitionierte Projekte wie die Stalinallee (seit 1961 Karl-Marx-Allee), eine Magistrale nach sowjetischem Vorbild. Architekt Hermann Henselmann stellte hier gekonnt Beziehungen zur Berliner Bautradition her, zu Schinkels Klassizismus und Gontards Türmen am Gendarmenmarkt.

In den 1970er Jahren schenkte man auf westlicher Seite der Altbausubstanz und der Schließung im Stadtbild klaffender Lücken besondere Aufmerksamkeit. Nachdem die jüngere Vergangenheit noch den Flächenabriss der alten Mietskasernen befördert hatte, begann nun die dichte Bebauung mit sanierten, aufgewerteten Mietshäusern zum Inbegriff städtischer Atmosphäre zu werden. Mit diesem im Westteil entwickelten Konzept der „Kritischen Rekonstruktion" ist die historische Stadt repariert worden, verstärkt auch seit dem Fall der Mauer im ehemaligen Ostteil. Auf dem historischen Stadtgrundriss orientieren sich Neubauten heute an der Größe der Altbauten, mitunter auch an deren Stil. Ganze Straßenzüge und Plätze, so der Pariser und der Leipziger Platz, werden auf diese Weise wiederhergestellt.

Ein neuer Publikumsmagnet ist der Potsdamer Platz, der auf eigene Weise an den Mythos der dynamischen Weltstadt von einst anknüpfen und Urbanität vermitteln will. Auch das politische Berlin hat neue Bauten geschaffen – die Ministerien, Ländervertretungen, Botschaften und das neue Regierungszentrum mit dem Bundeskanzleramt. Und im Umgang mit dem historischen Bauerbe hat sich die Demokratie als kluge Bauherrin erwiesen. So ist der Reichstag mit seiner spektakulären Kuppel nicht nur viel besuchtes Ziel politisch und architektonisch Interessierter, sondern auch Wahrzeichen des „neuen Berlin" geworden, in dem sich Gegenwart und Zukunft vereinen.

Die Metropole hat sich in den letzten Jahren eine neue Silhouette gegeben. Auch dieser Band ist deshalb nur eine Momentaufnahme, denn ganz sicher sieht die Stadt in zehn Jahren schon wieder anders aus. Doch womöglich gelingt es auch, den traditionellen Hang zur Traditionslosigkeit zu überwinden und endgültig das architektonische Erbe Berlins mit dem dynamischen Geist der Metropole zu versöhnen.

thoroughfare based on the Soviet model. Here, architect Hermann Henselmann skilfully related his work to Berlin's architectural traditions, to Schinkel's classicism and Gontard's towers on the Gendarmenmarkt.

In the 1970s, planners in West Berlin paid more attention to the architectural fabric and to closing yawning gaps in the urban landscape.

Dense development with renovated, upgraded blocks of flats now started to become the epitome of urban atmosphere, replacing the hitherto support for extensive demolition of old tenement blocks. The historical city was repaired using this concept of critical reconstruction developed in the Western part. It has also been used increasingly in the former East since the fall of the Wall. Now, new buildings are aligned towards the city's historical ground plans in terms of the size of the old buildings – and occasionally their style too. In this way, whole streets and squares are being recreated, such as Pariser Platz and Leipziger Platz.

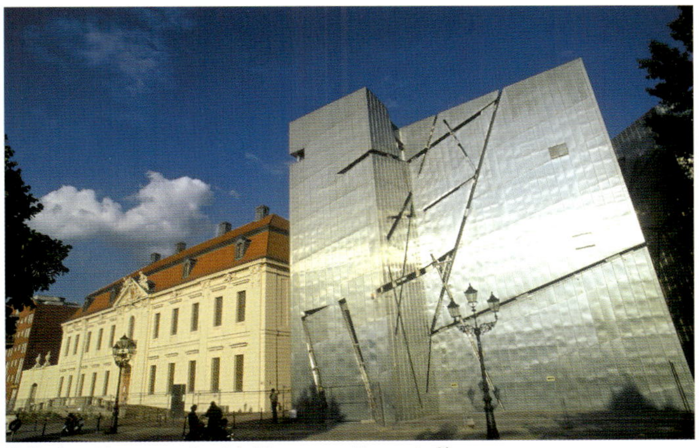

Jüdisches Museum • Jewish Museum • Museo Judío

Potsdamer Platz is one new crowd-puller aiming to link up with the old myth of the dynamic metropolis in its own way and convey urbanity. Political Berlin has also created numerous new buildings – the ministries, Länder representatives, embassies and the new government centre with the Federal Chancellery. In addition, democracy has proven to be a clever developer in its treatment of the heritage of historical buildings. In this sense, the Reichstag, the rebuilt German parliament building, with its spectacular dome has become not just a much-visited destination for those interested in politics and architecture, but also the symbol of the New Berlin, one uniting the present and future.

In the last few years, the metropolis has given itself a new silhouette. For this reason, this book is just a record of the present. In ten years time, the city will certainly look very different once again. However, it might just be possible that by then the traditional tendency towards an absence of tradition will have been successfully overcome and the architectonic inheritance of Berlin finally reconciled with the dynamic spirit of the metropolis.

modelo soviético. El arquitecto Hermann Henselmann enlazó aquí magistralmente la tradición arquitectónica berlinesa, con el clasicismo de Schinkel y con las torres de Gontard en el Gendarmenmarkt.

En la zona occidental se dedicó en los años 70 del siglo pasado una atención especial a la materia antigua y al cierre de espacios abiertos en el paisaje urbano.

Después de que en el pasado reciente todavía se habían fomentado los derribos de los antiguos bloques de viviendas, la densa edificación con bloques de viviendas saneadas y revalorizadas comenzaba ahora a convertirse en la esencia de la atmósfera urbana. Con este concepto de «reconstrucción crítica», desarrollado en la zona occidental, la ciudad histórica fue restaurada, lo que también se dio intensamente en la antigua zona oriental desde la caída del Muro. Los nuevos edificios de la zona histórica de la ciudad se orientan hoy en día a la grandeza de los edificios antiguos y, de vez en cuando, tambien a su estilo. De esta manera se reconstruyen sectores enteros de calles y plazas como la Pariser Platz y la Leipziger Platz.

Un nuevo imán para el púbico es la Postdamer Platz la cual quiere, de un modo propio, enlazar con el mito de la metrópoli dinámica de antaño y comunicar urbanidad. El Berlín político también ha creado numerosos edificios nuevos: los ministerios, las representaciones de los Länder, las Embajadas y el nuevo centro de gobierno con el edificio de la cancillería. Y en el trato con la herencia arquitectónica histórica la democracia se ha evidenciado como una constructora sensata. Así el Reichstag, con su espectacular cúpula se ha convertido no solamente en un objetivo muy visitado por quienes se interesan por la política y la arquitectura sino también en el símbolo del «nuevo» Berlín donde se unen el presente y el futuro.

En los últimos años, la metrópoli se ha dado a sí misma una nueva silueta. Por eso, este libro recoge sólamente un momento ya que, con toda seguridad, dentro de diez años la ciudad de nuevo tendrá otro aspecto. Pero a lo mejor también se consigue superar la tradicional tendencia a la falta de tradición y conciliar definitivamente la herencia arquitectónica de Berlín con el espíritu dinámico de la metrópoli.

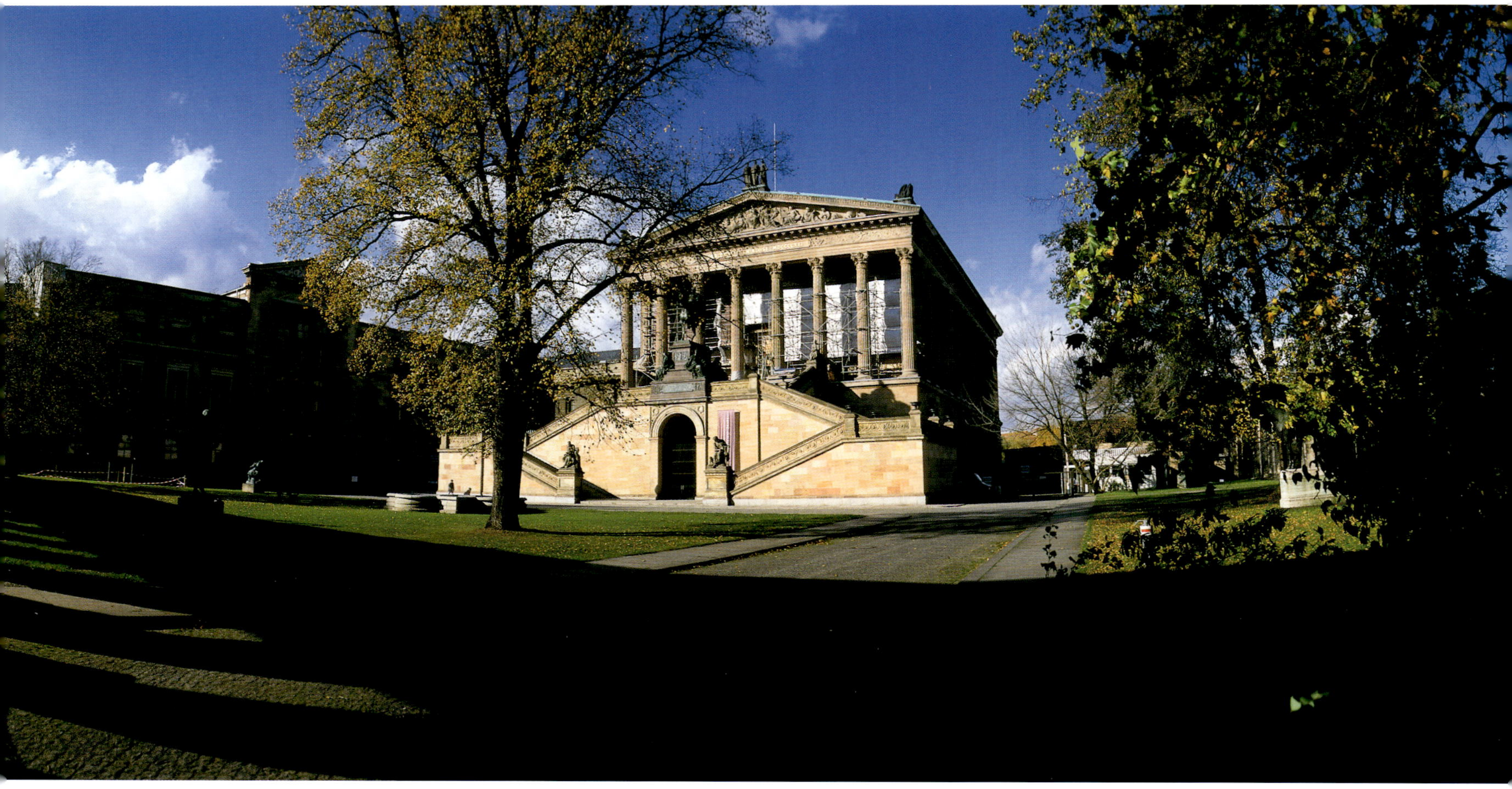

Alte Nationalgalerie
Friedrich August Stüler
(Entwurf · original design · proyecto),
Johann Heinrich Strack
(Ausführung · realisation · realización)
1866–1867
H.G. Merz
(Umbau · alteration · reforma)
1992–2001
Bodestraße
Museum · museum · museo

Altes Museum mit · with · con Lustgarten
Karl Friedrich Schinkel
1824–1828
Lustgarten
Museum · museum · museo

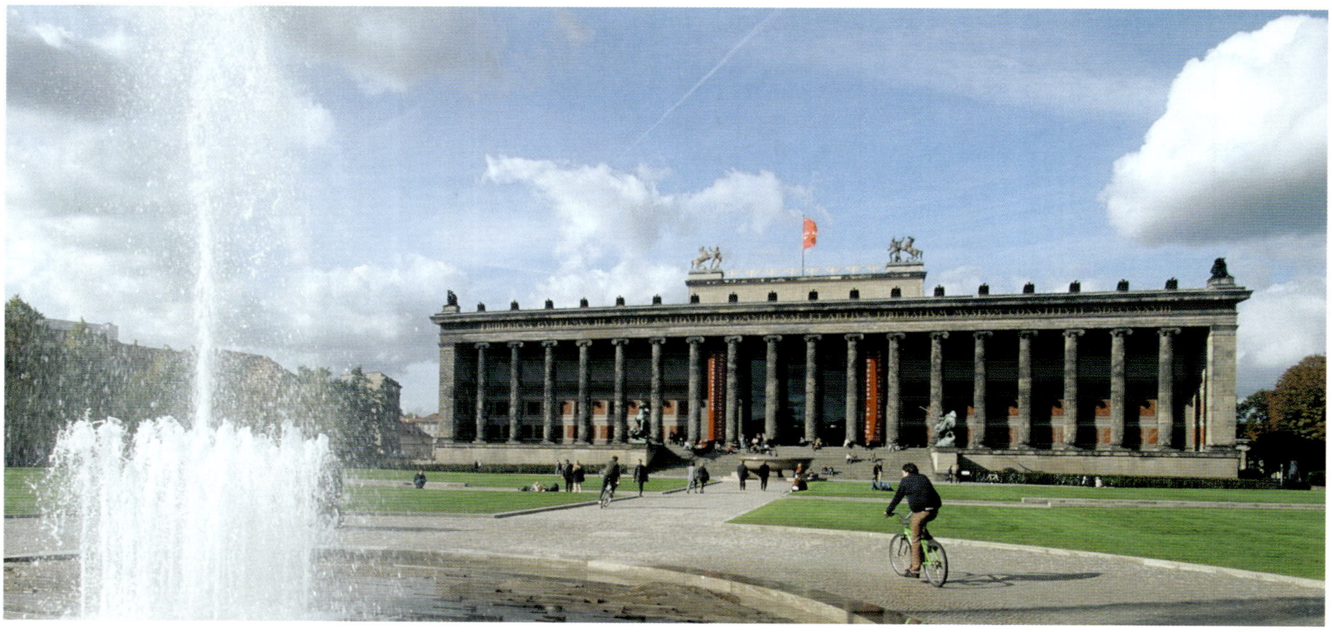

Bodemuseum
(im Hintergrund Fernsehturm
in the background television tower
Torre de la Televisón al fondo)
Ernst von Ihne
1897–1904
Am Kupfergraben
Museum · museum · museo

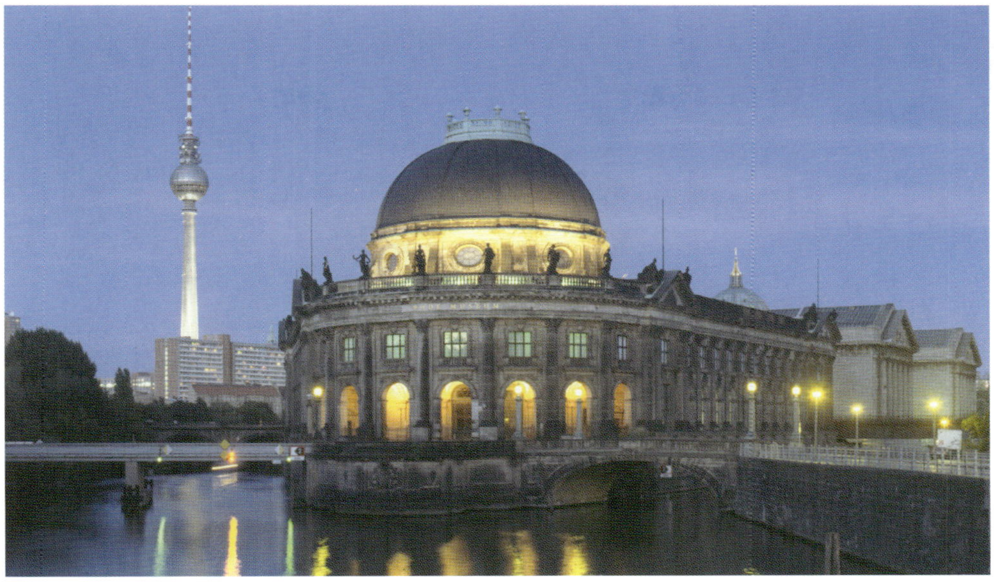

Staatsoper
Unter den Linden
Georg Wenzeslaus von Knobelsdorff, Karl Ferdinand Langhans, Richard Paulick
1741–1743, 1788, 1952–1955
Unter den Linden
Opernhaus · opera house · opera

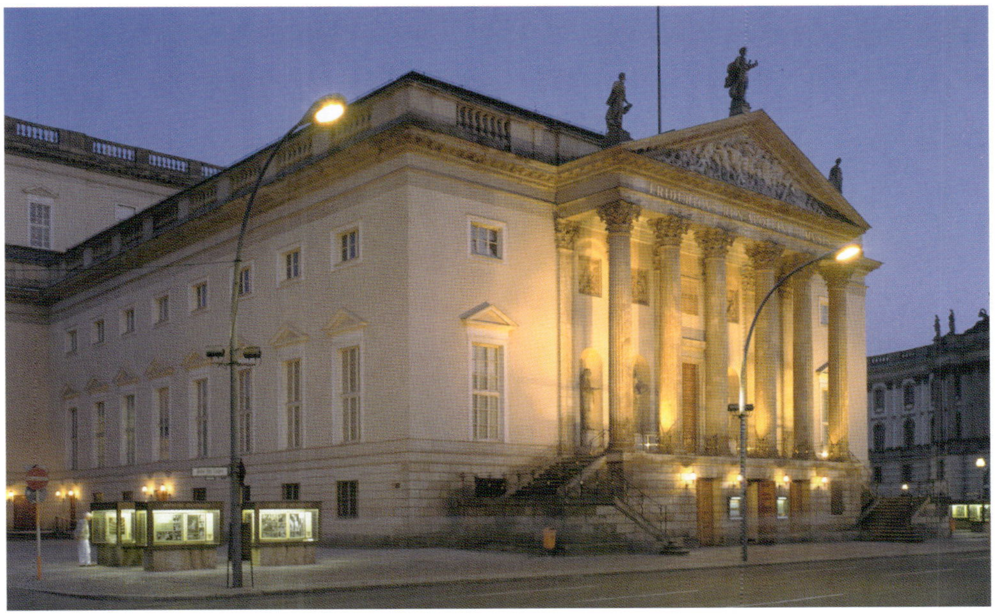

Brandenburger Tor
Brandenburg Gate
Puerta de Brandenburgo
Carl Gotthard Langhans
1788–1791
Pariser Platz

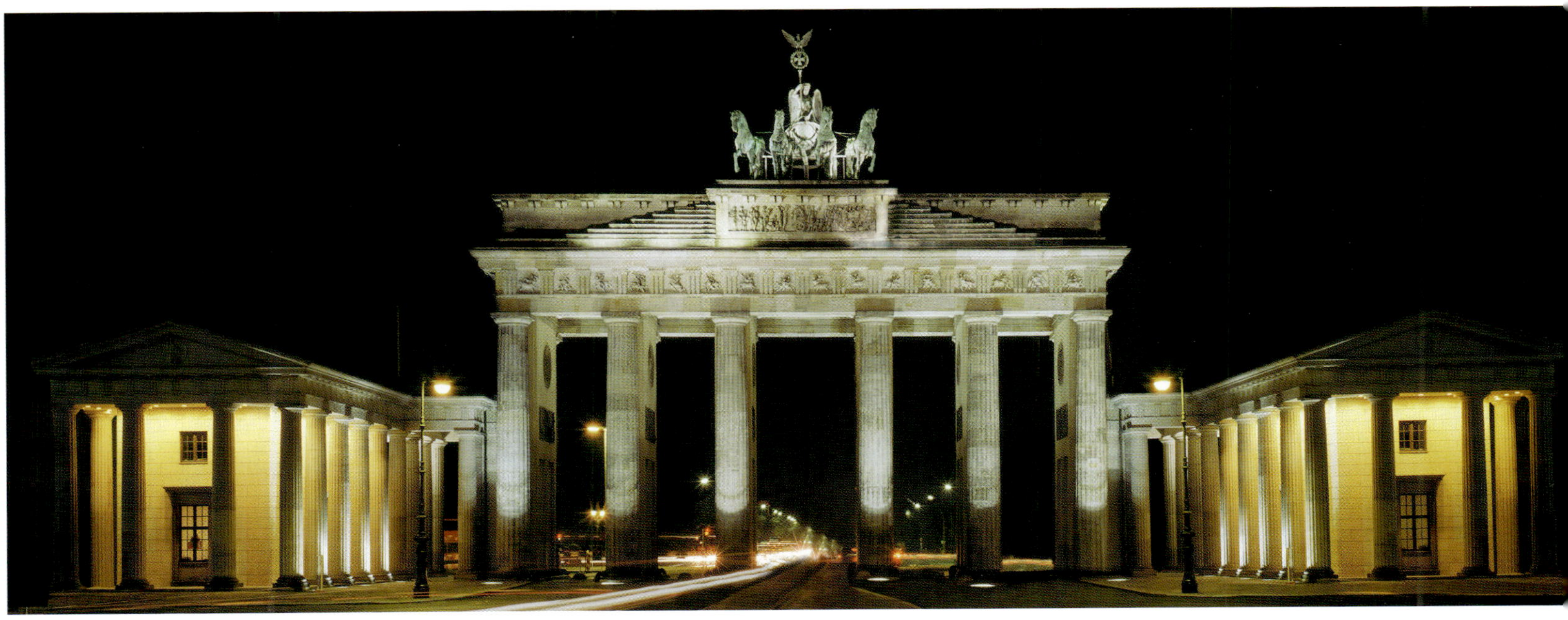

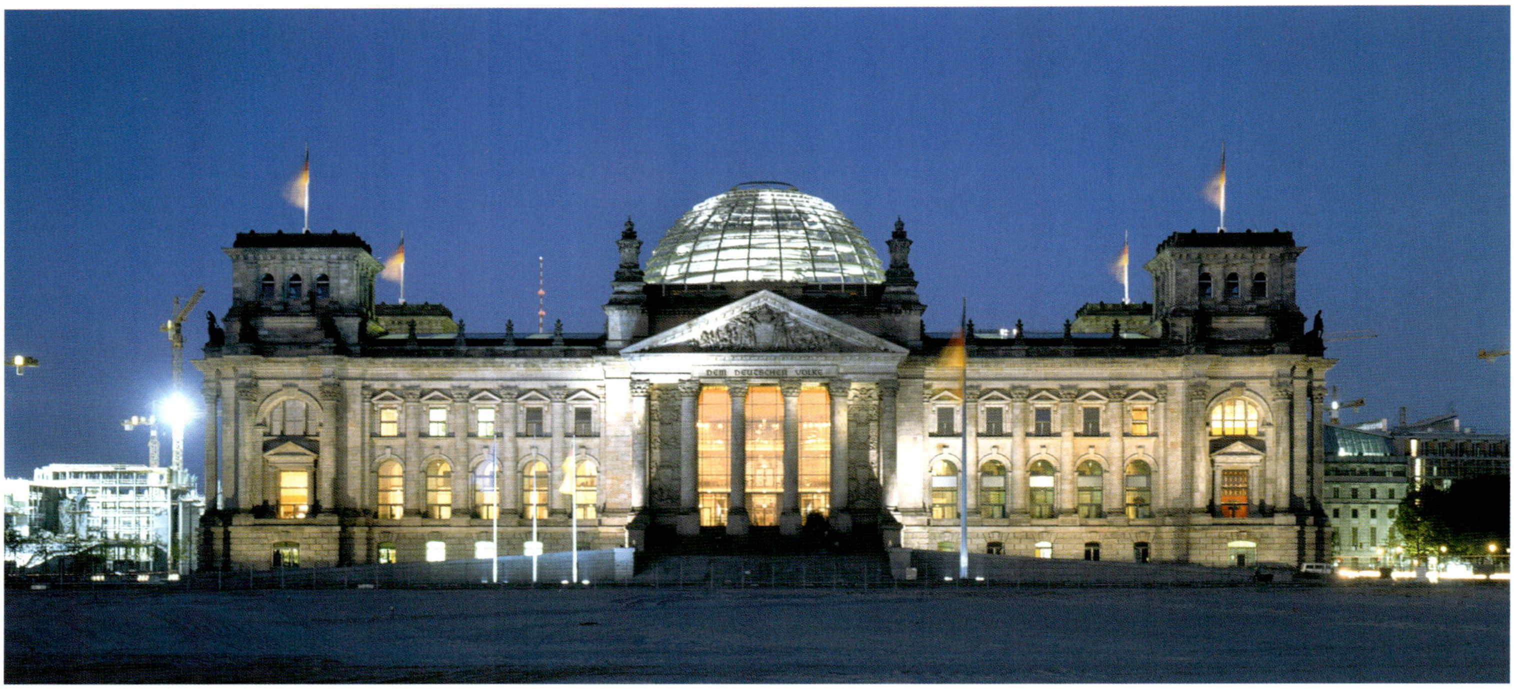

Reichstag
Paul Wallot, Norman Foster
1884–1894, 1995–1999
Platz der Republik
Sitz des Deutschen Bundestages
Seat of the German Federal Parliament
Sede del Parlamento Federal

Bundeskanzleramt
The Federal Chancellery
Cancillería Federal
Axel Schultes Architekten,
Frank, Schultes, Witt
(Axel Schultes mit · with · con
Charlotte Frank), Berlin
1997–2001
Willy-Brandt Straße

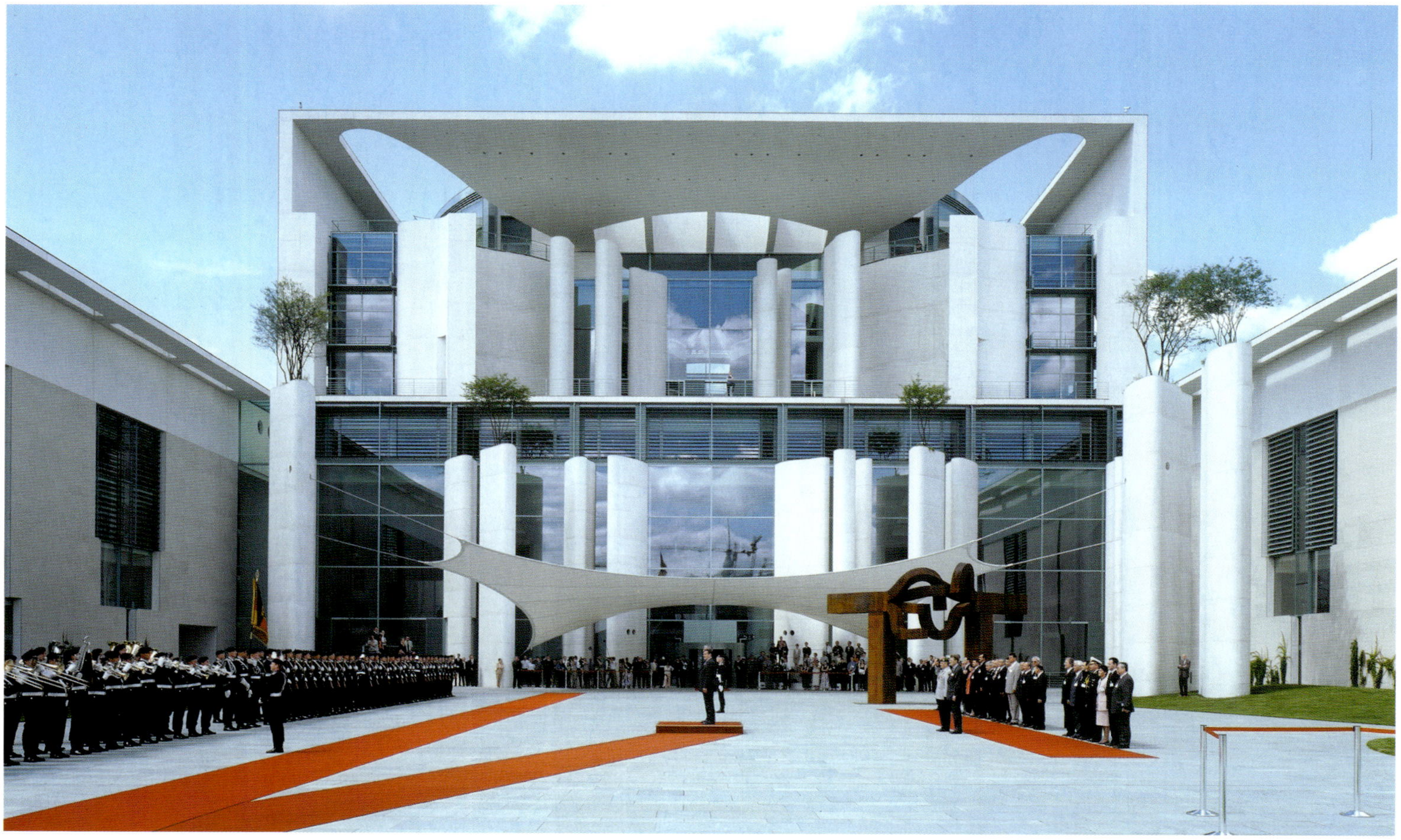

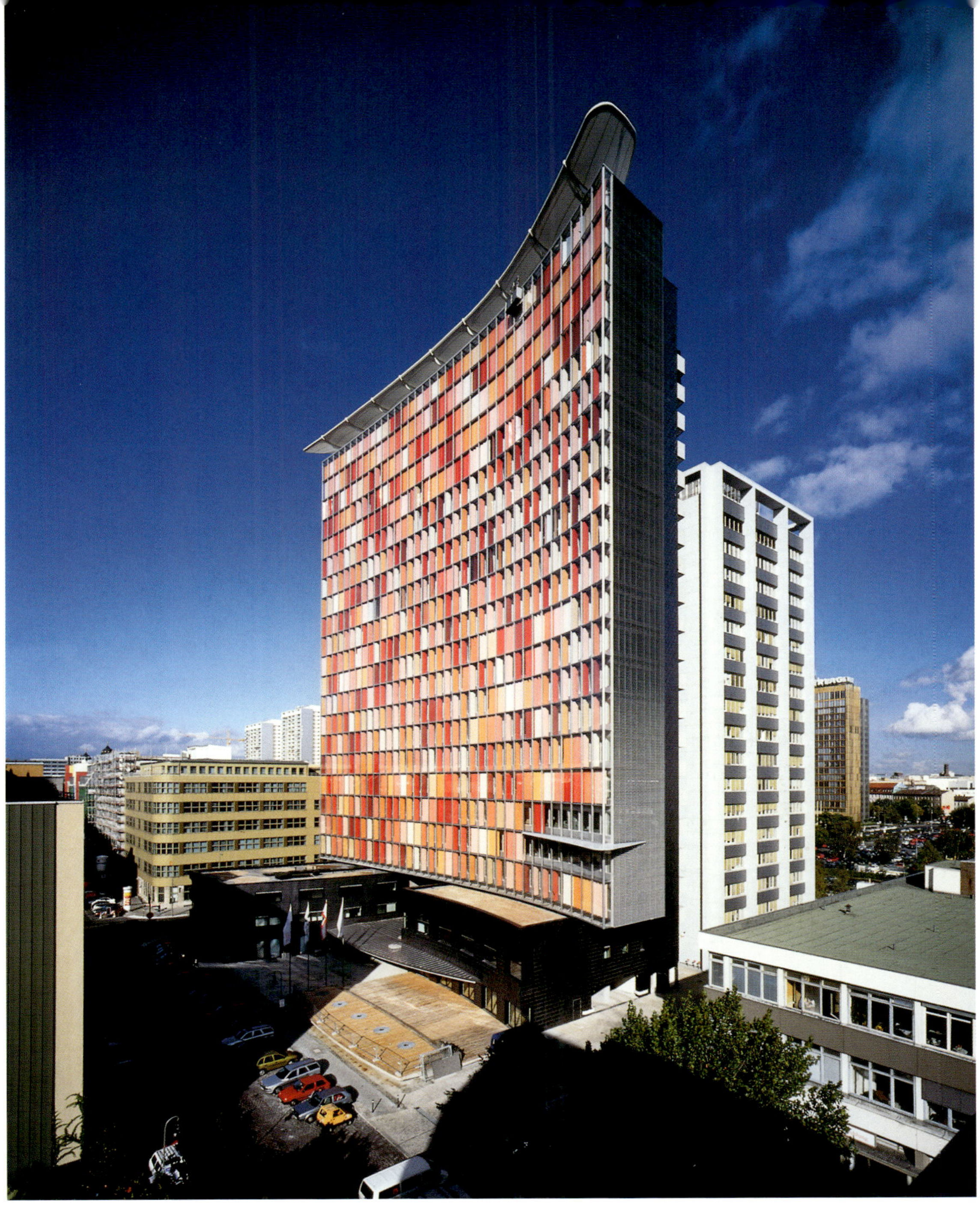

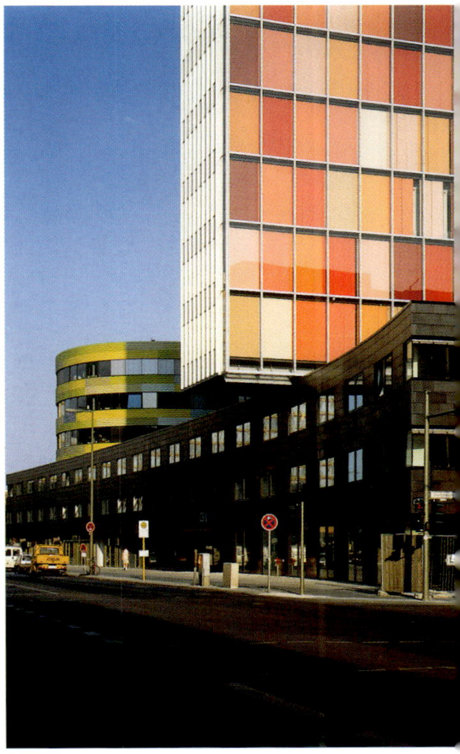

Erweiterung GSW-Gebäude
Sauerbruch Hutton, Berlin/London
1995–1998
Kochstraße
Büro, Gewerbe
Office, business
Oficinas, comercio

Redaktionsgebäude der »tageszeitung«
Gerhard Spangenberg (mit · with · con Brigitte Steinkilberg, Berlin)
1988–1990
Kochstraße
Büro, Gewerbe
Office, business
Oficinas, comercio

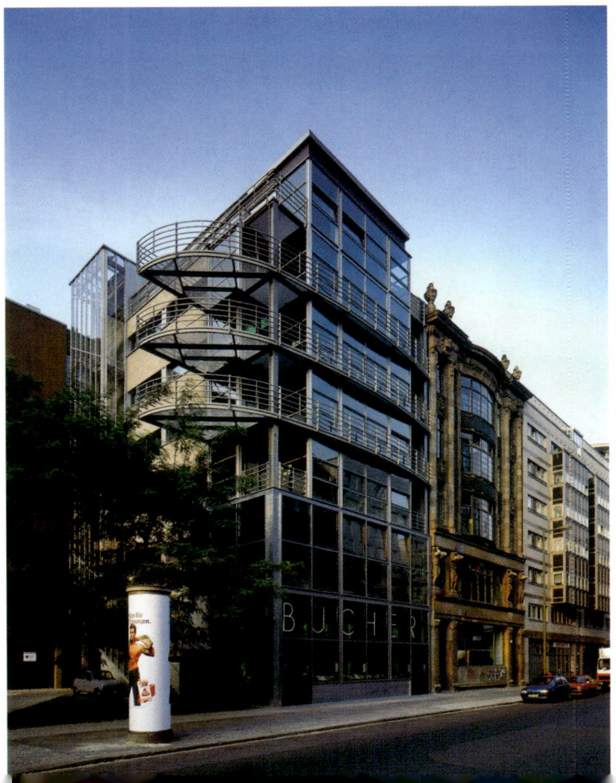

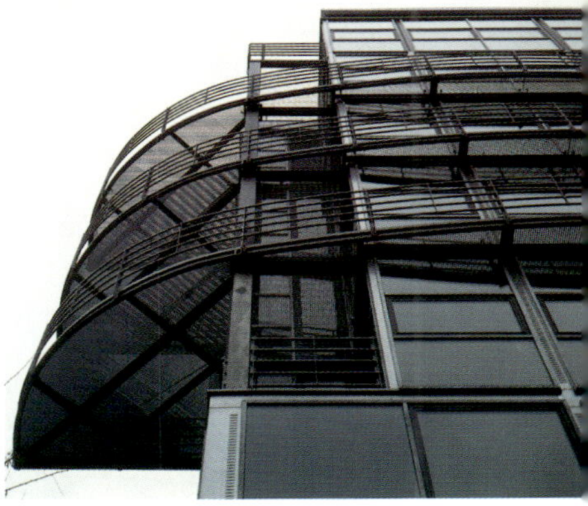

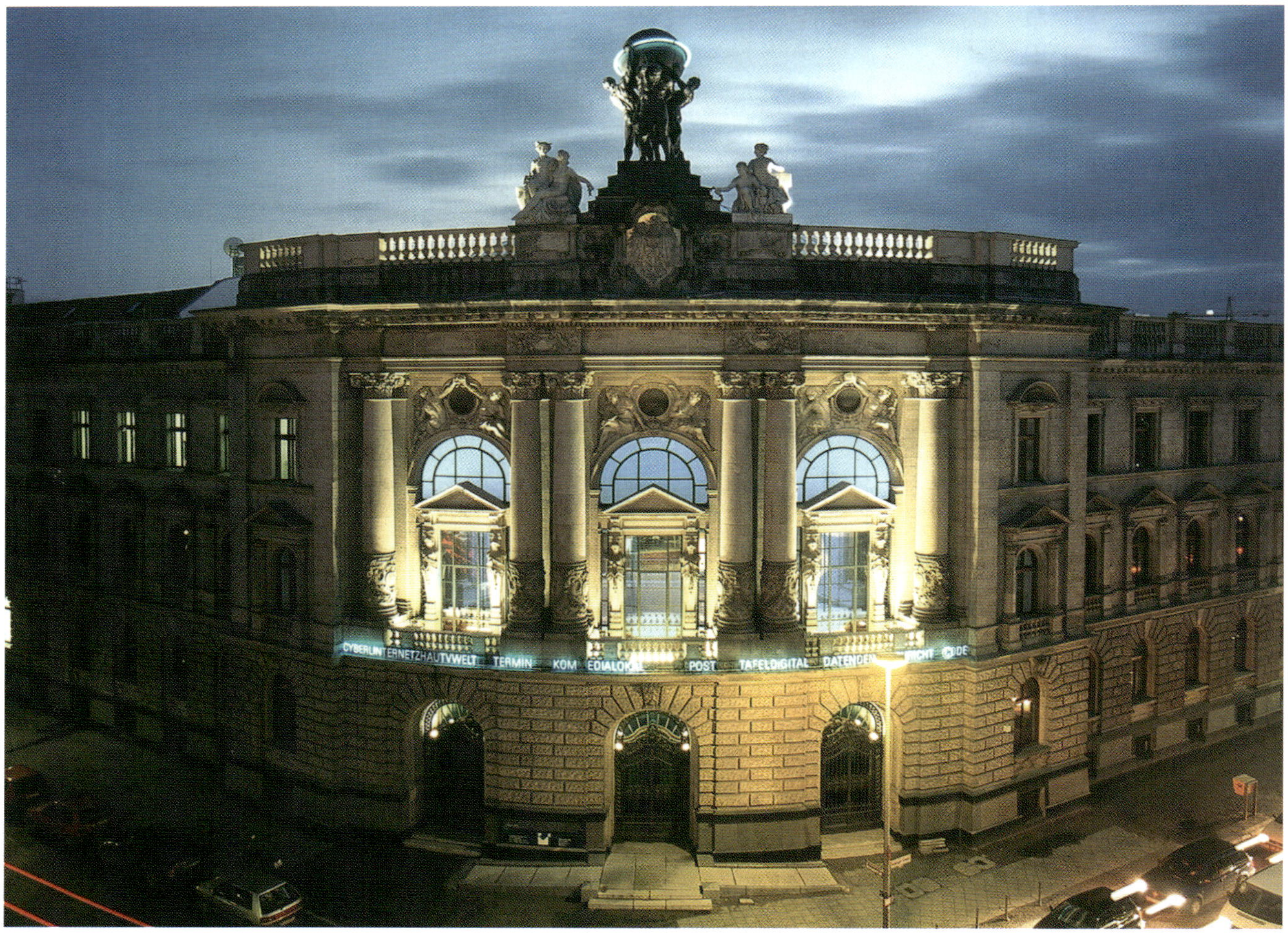

Ehemaliges Reichspostmuseum
Ernst Hake, Heinrich Techow, Franz Ahrens
1893–1897
Leipziger Straße · Mauerstraße
Museum für Kommunikation Berlin
Communications Museum
Museo de la Comunicación

Ehemaliges Reichsluftfahrtministerium
Former Reich Air Travel Ministry
Antiguo Ministerio de Aviación del Reich
Ernst Sagebiel (Altbau · old building · edificio original),
Hentrich-Petschnigg & Partner (HPP), Berlin
(Umbau · alteration · reforma)
1935–1936
1994–1999
Leipziger Straße · Wilhelmstraße
Bundesministerium für Finanzen
Federal Ministry of Finance
Ministerio Federal de Hacienda

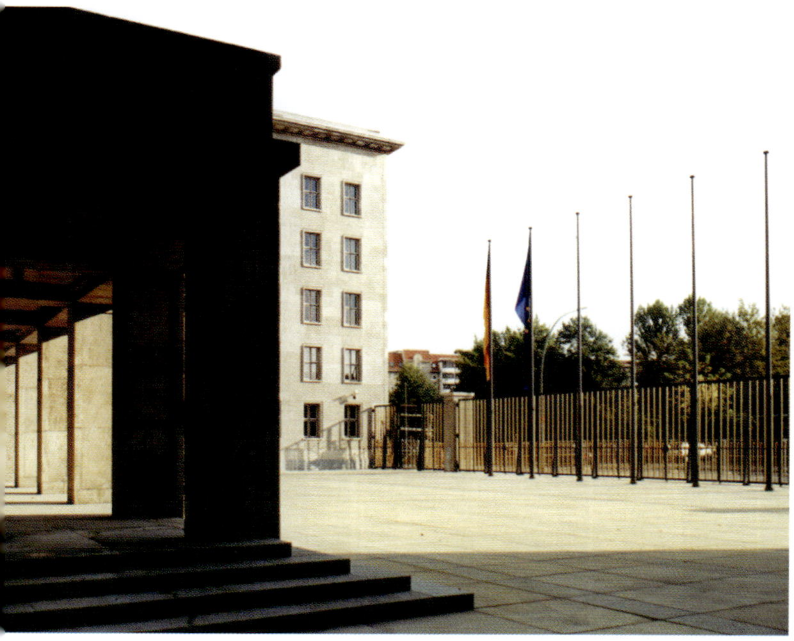

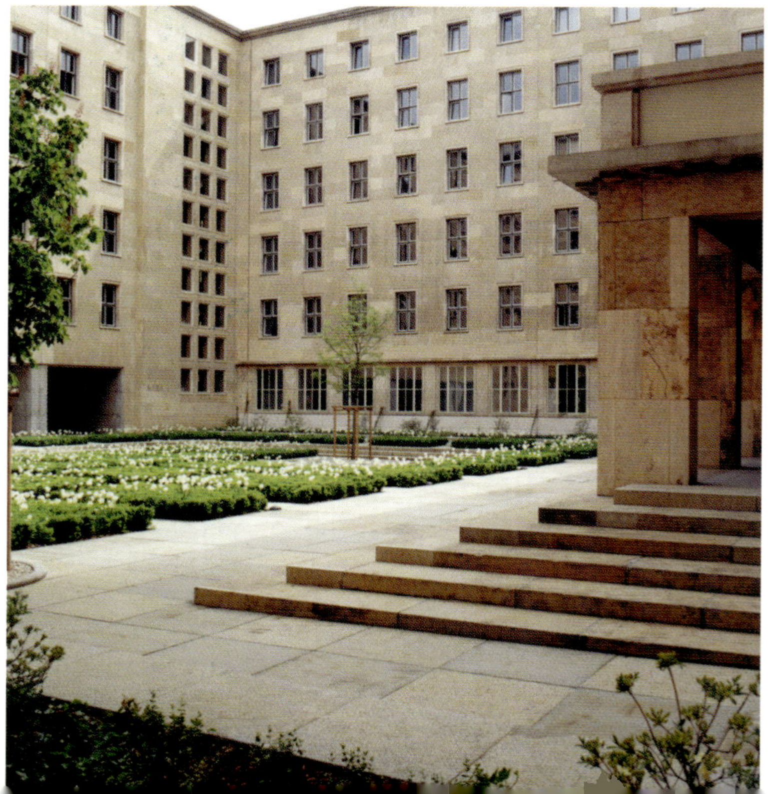

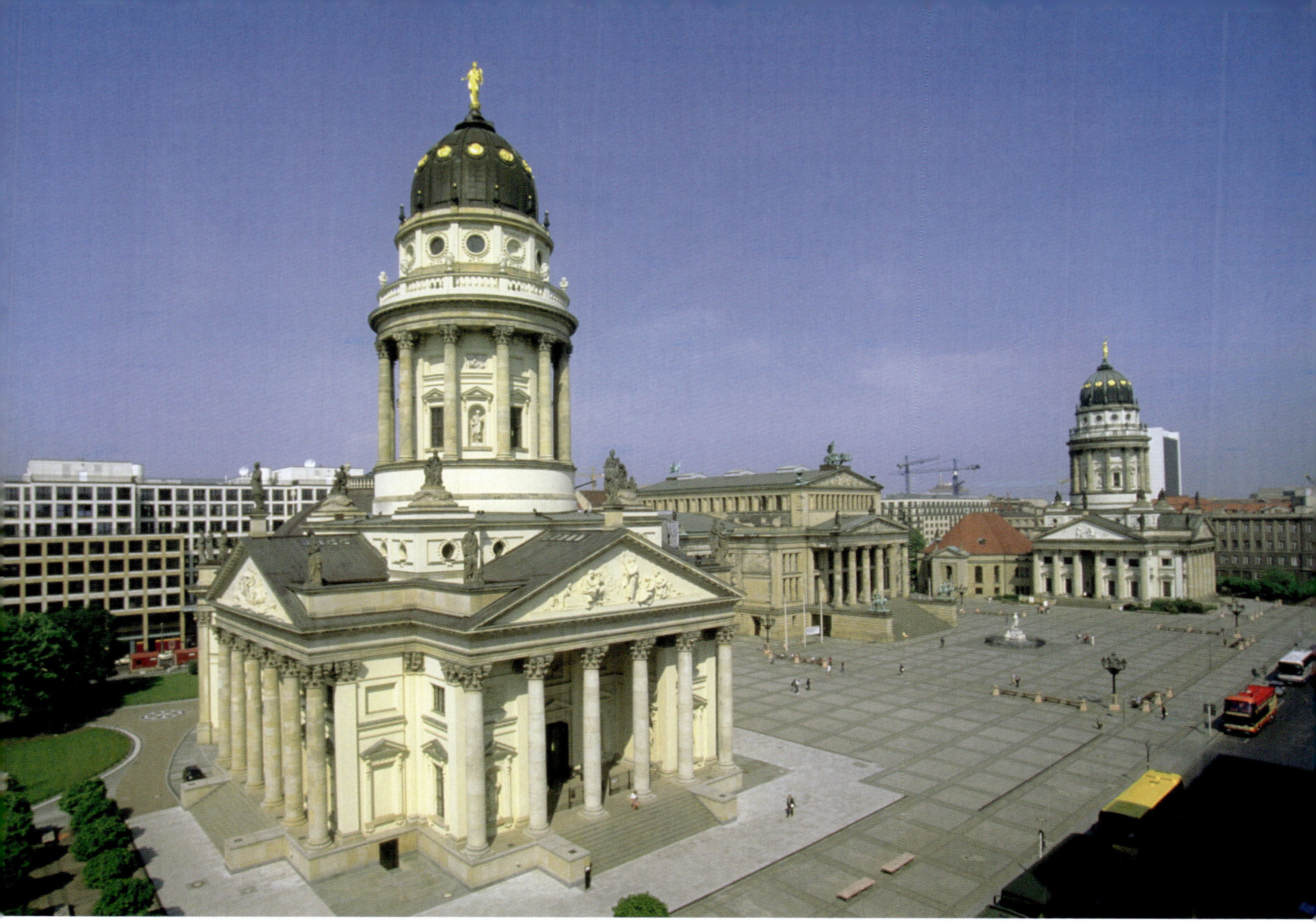

Gendarmenmarkt mit Deutscher (links · left · izquierda) und Französischer Kirche (rechts · right · derecha) und Schauspielhaus (mitte · middle · centro)
Martin Grünberg, Giovanni Simonetti,
Louis Cayard, Abraham Quesnays,
Karl von Gontard (Deutsche und Französische Kirche),
Karl Friedrich Schinkel (Schauspielhaus)
1701–1705/08, 1780–1785
(Deutsche und Französische Kirche),
1818–1821 (Schauspielhaus)
Gendarmenmarkt
Ausstellungsort, Gewerbe, Kirche, Konzertsaal
Exhibition hall, business, church, concert hall
Sala de exposiciones, comercio, iglesia, sala de conciertos

BEWAG-Haus
Max Dudler, Zürich/Berlin
(mit · with · con Manfred Kunz
und · and · y Brigitta Weise)
1994–1997
Markgrafenstraße
Büro, Gewerbe, Wohnen
Office, business, residence
Oficinas, comercio, viviendas

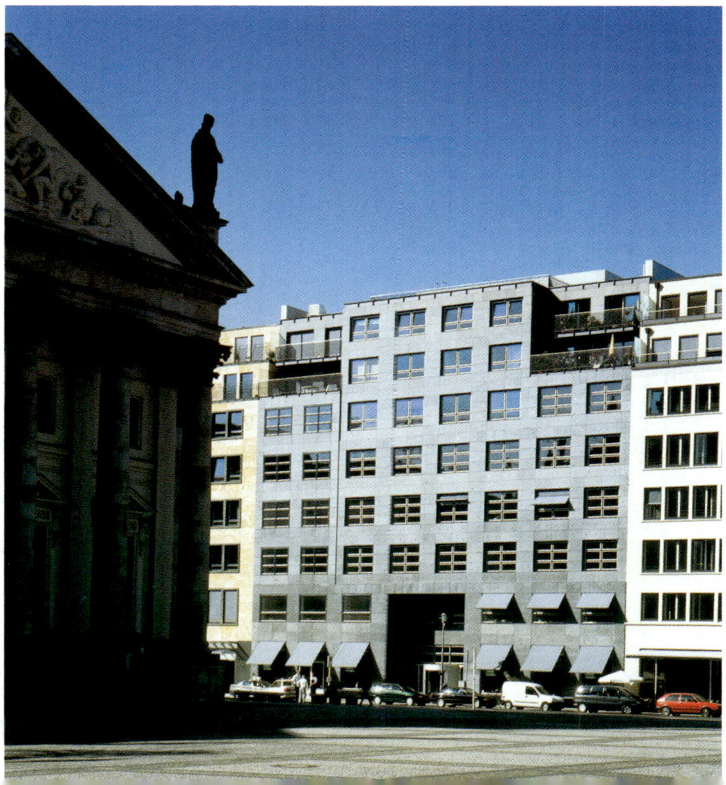

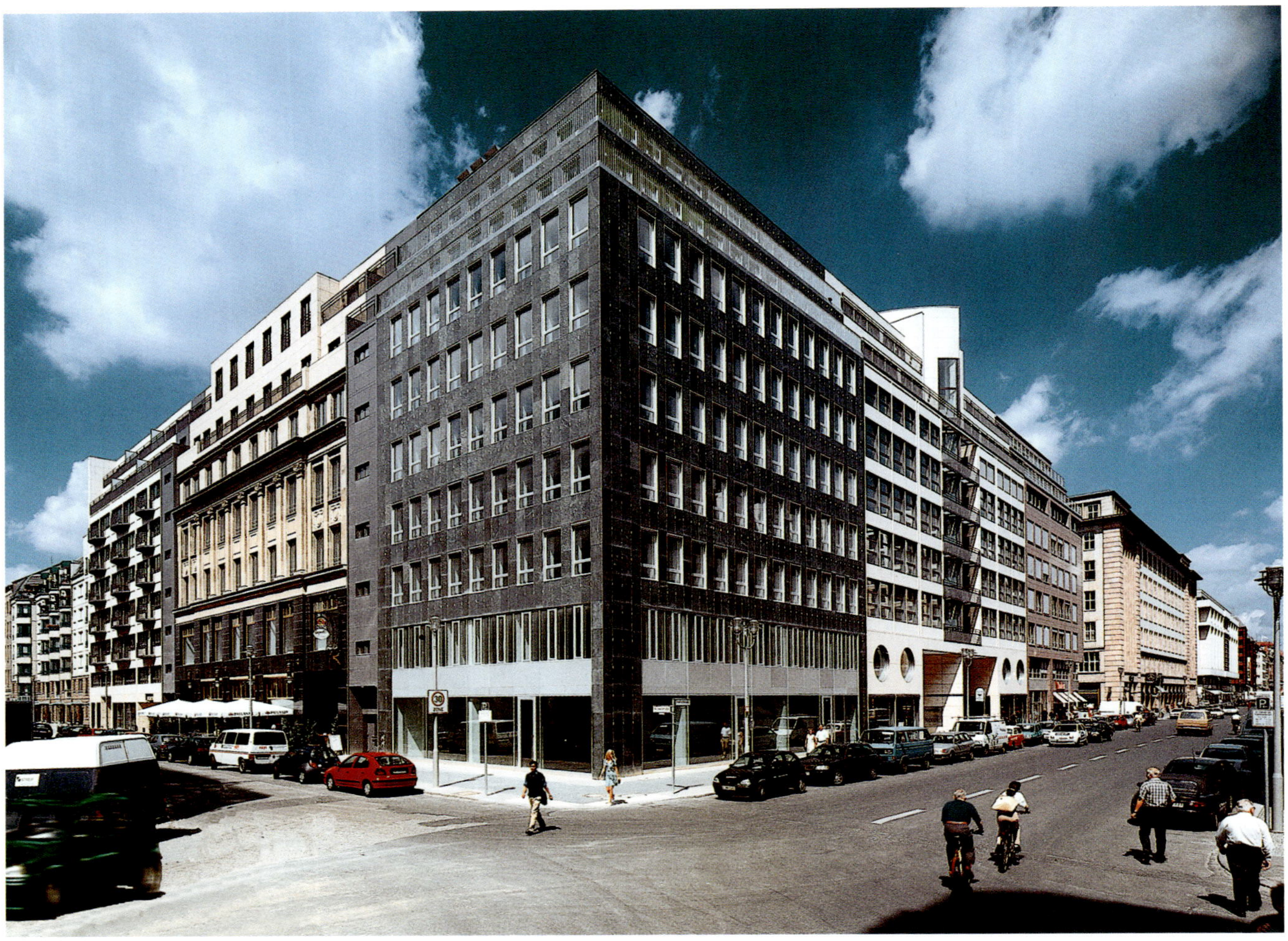

Kontorhaus Mitte
Josef Paul Kleihues, Berlin,
Klaus Theo Brenner, Berlin,
Vittorio Magnago Lampugnani
mit · with · con Marlene Dörrie,
Frankfurt a. M.,
Walther Stepp, Berlin
1994–1997
Friedrichstraße · Mohrenstraße
Büro, Gewerbe, Wohnen
Office, business, residence
Oficinas, comercio, viviendas

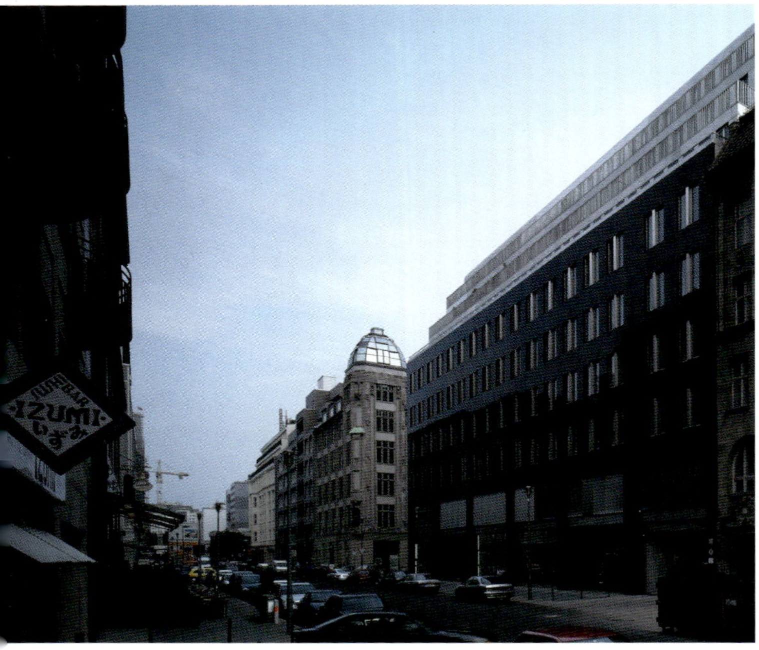

Quartier 108
Thomas van den Valentyn
mit · with · con Andreas Dittmann, Köln
1996–1998
Friedrichstraße · Leipziger Straße
Büro, Gewerbe, Wohnen
Office, business, residence
Oficinas, comercio, viviendas

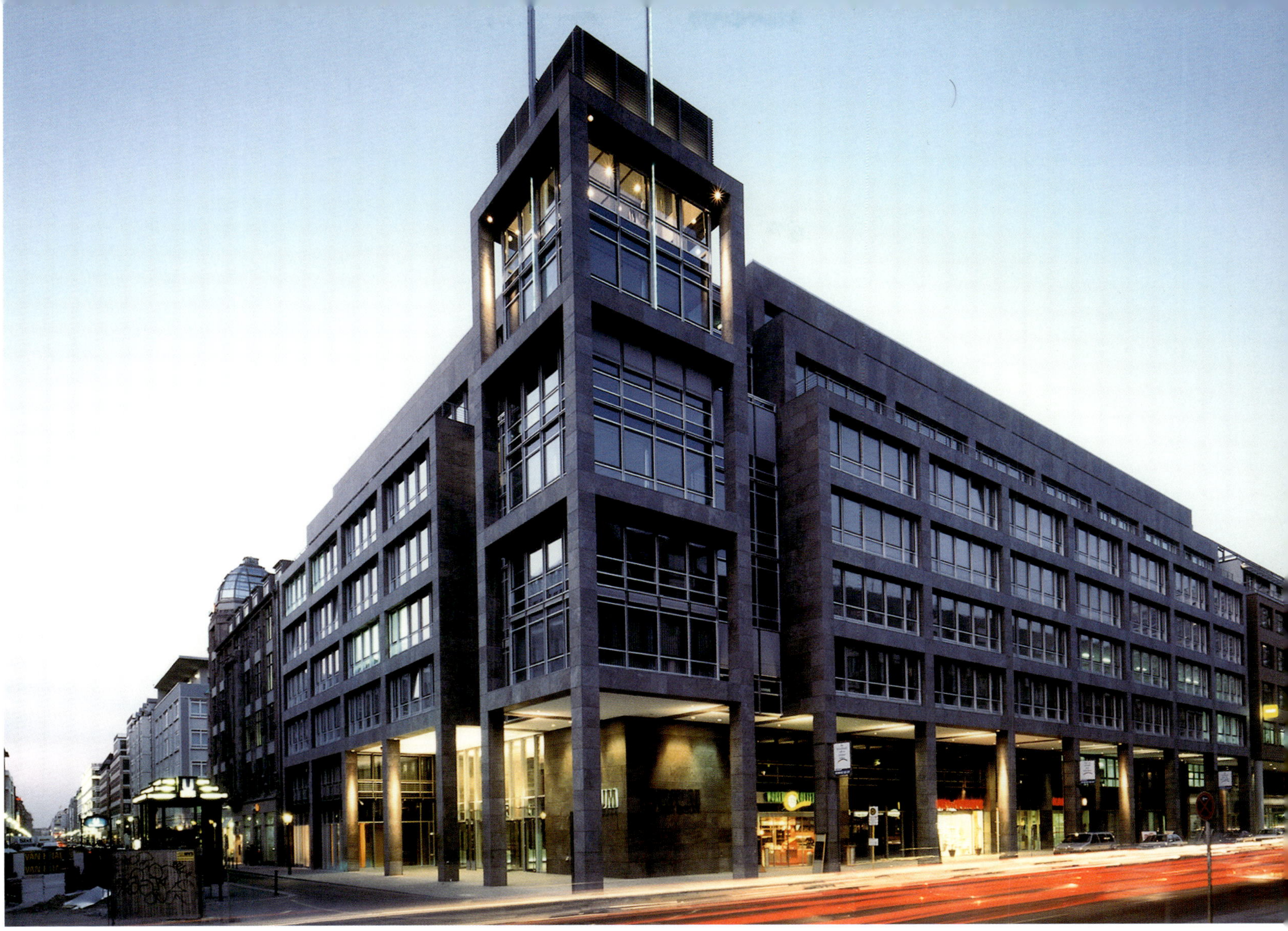

Atrium Friedrichstraße (Quartier 203)
gmp von Gerkan, Marg & Partner,
Generalplanung: ECE Projektmanagement, Hamburg
1995–1997
Friedrichstraße · Leipziger Straße
Büro, Gewerbe, Wohnen
Office, business, residence
Oficinas, comercio, viviendas

Friedrichstadt-Passagen (Quartier 205)
Oswald Mathias Ungers & Partner, Köln/Berlin
1992–1996
Friedrichstraße · Charlottenstraße · Mohrenstraße · Taubenstraße
Büro, Gewerbe, Wohnen
Office, business, residence
Oficinas, comercio, viviendas

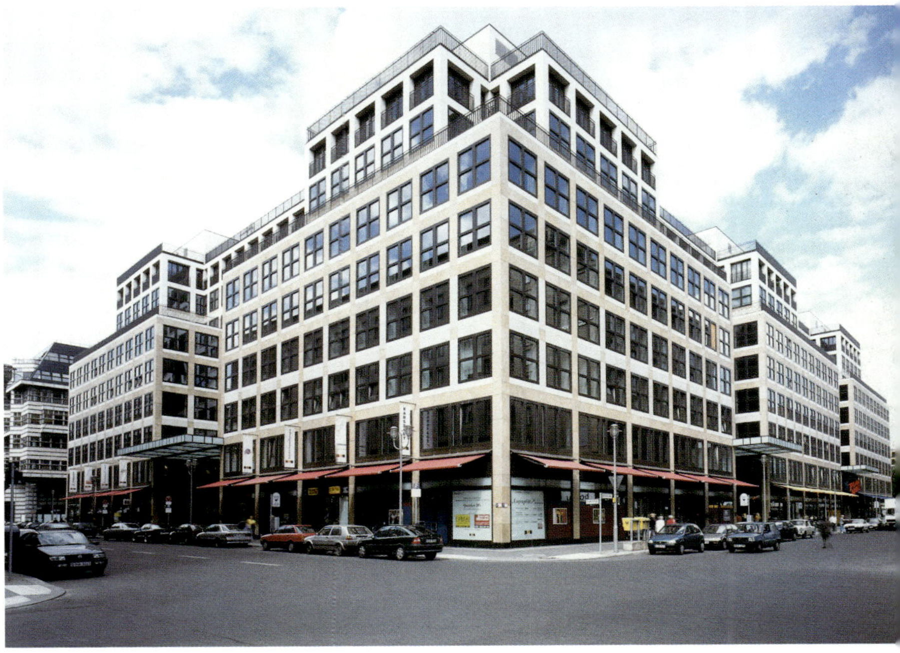

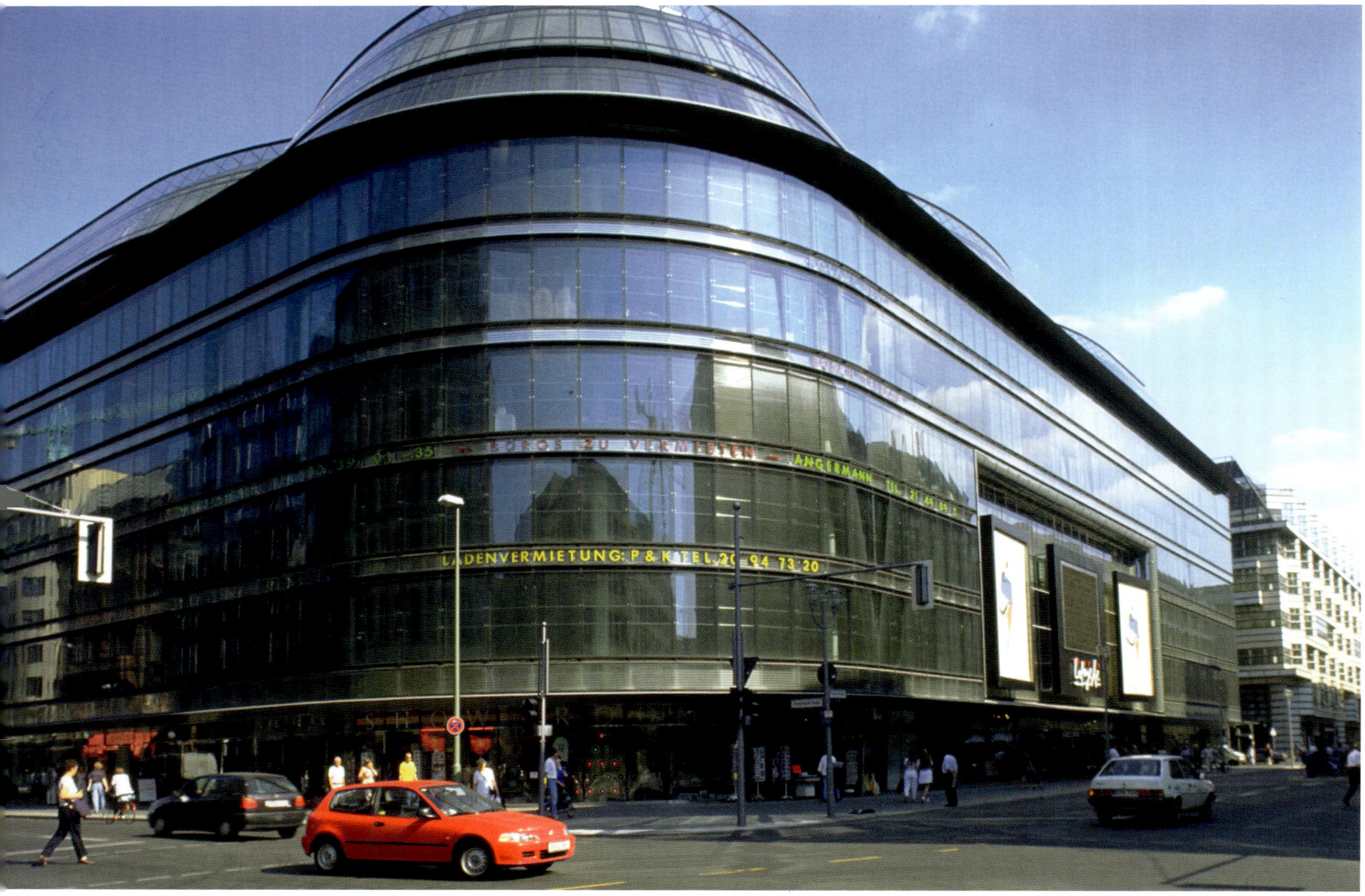

Friedrichstadt-Passagen
Galeries Lafayette (Quartier 207)
Jean Nouvel, Paris
1993–1996
Friedrichstraße
Büro, Gewerbe, Wohnen
Office, business, residence
Oficinas, comercio, viviendas

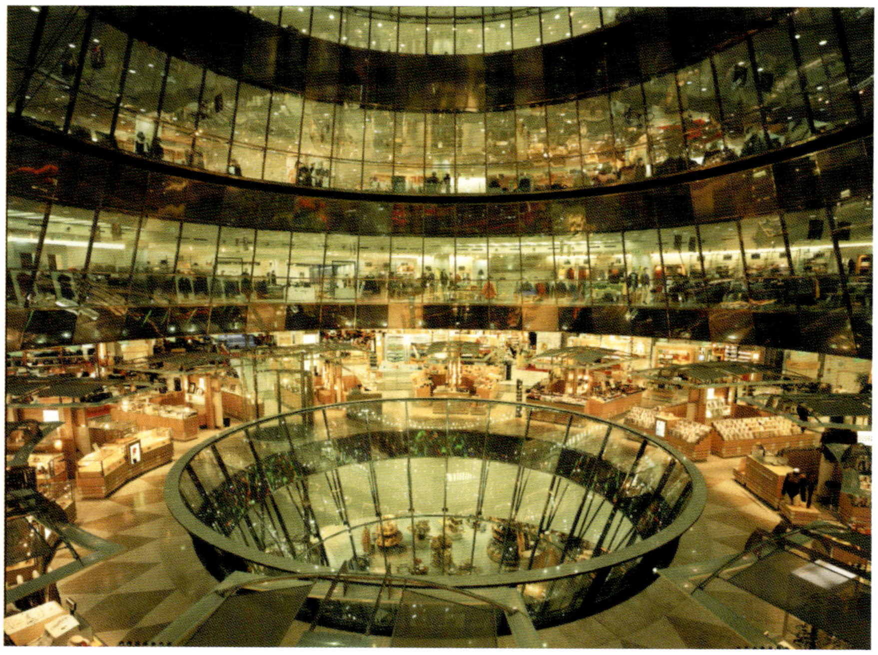

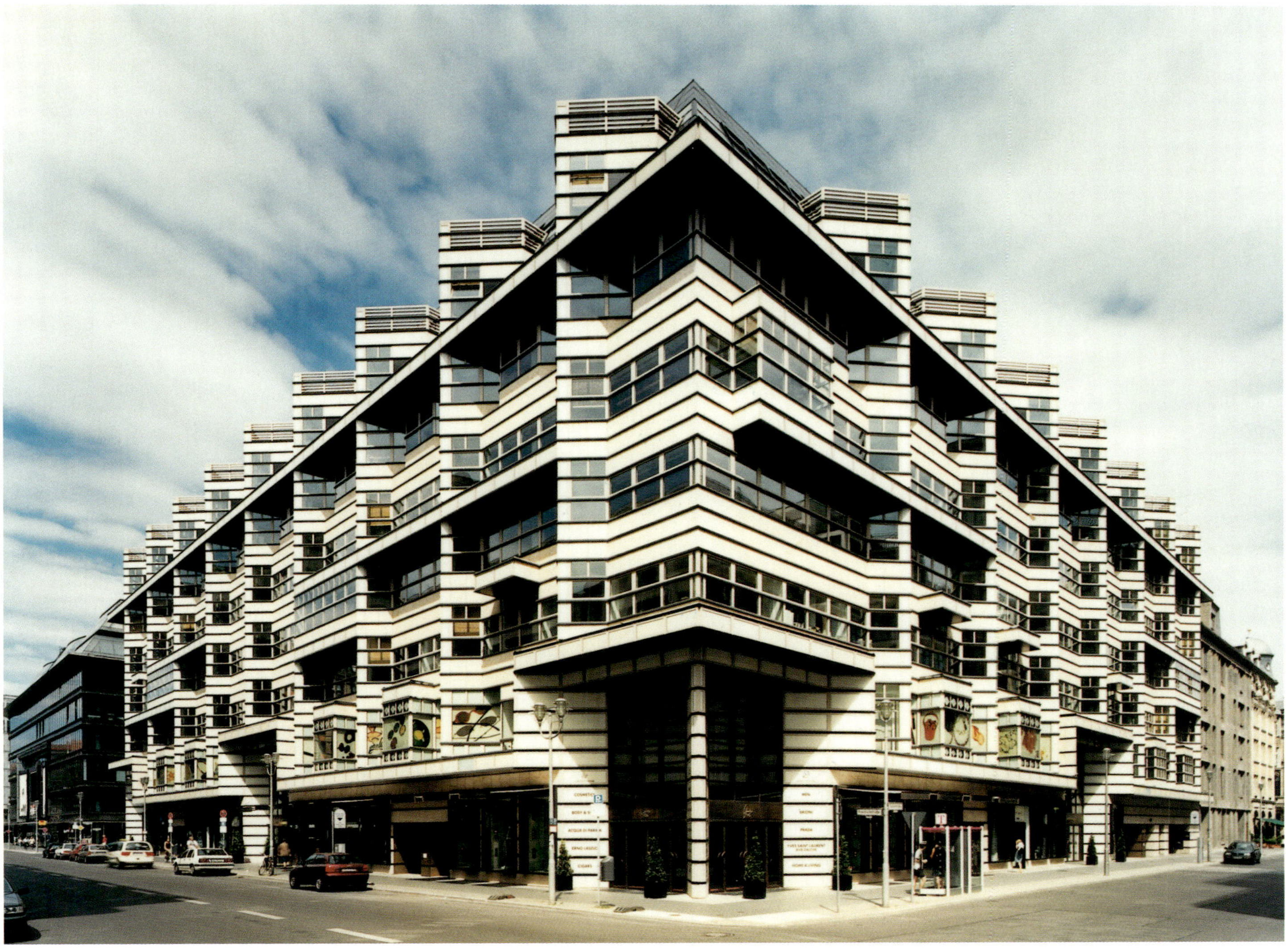

Friedrichstadt-Passagen (Quartier 206)
Pei, Cobb & Partners, New York
1992–1996
Friedrichstraße
Büro, Gewerbe, Wohnen · office, business, residence · oficinas, comercio, viviendas

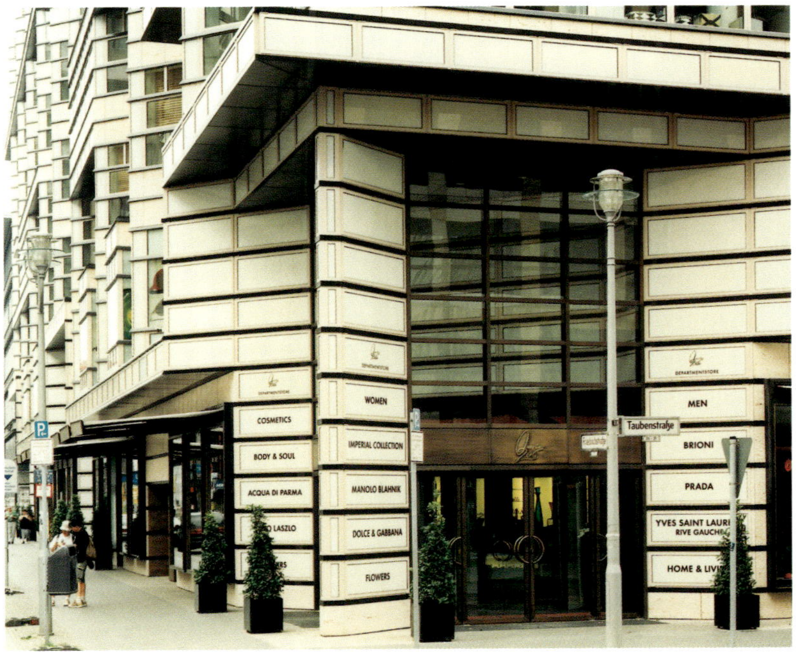

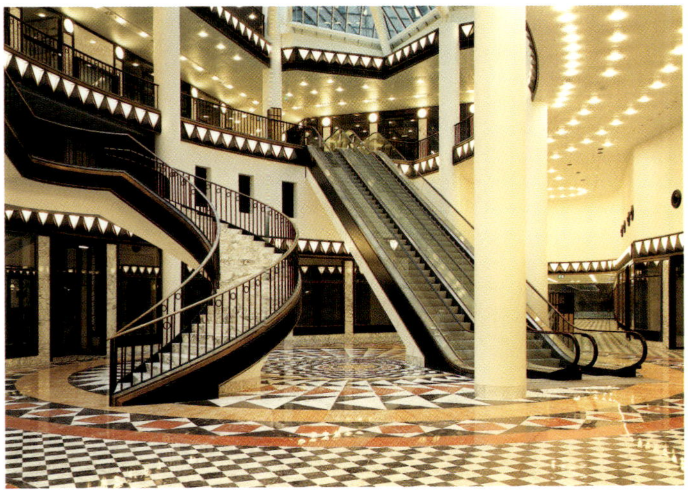

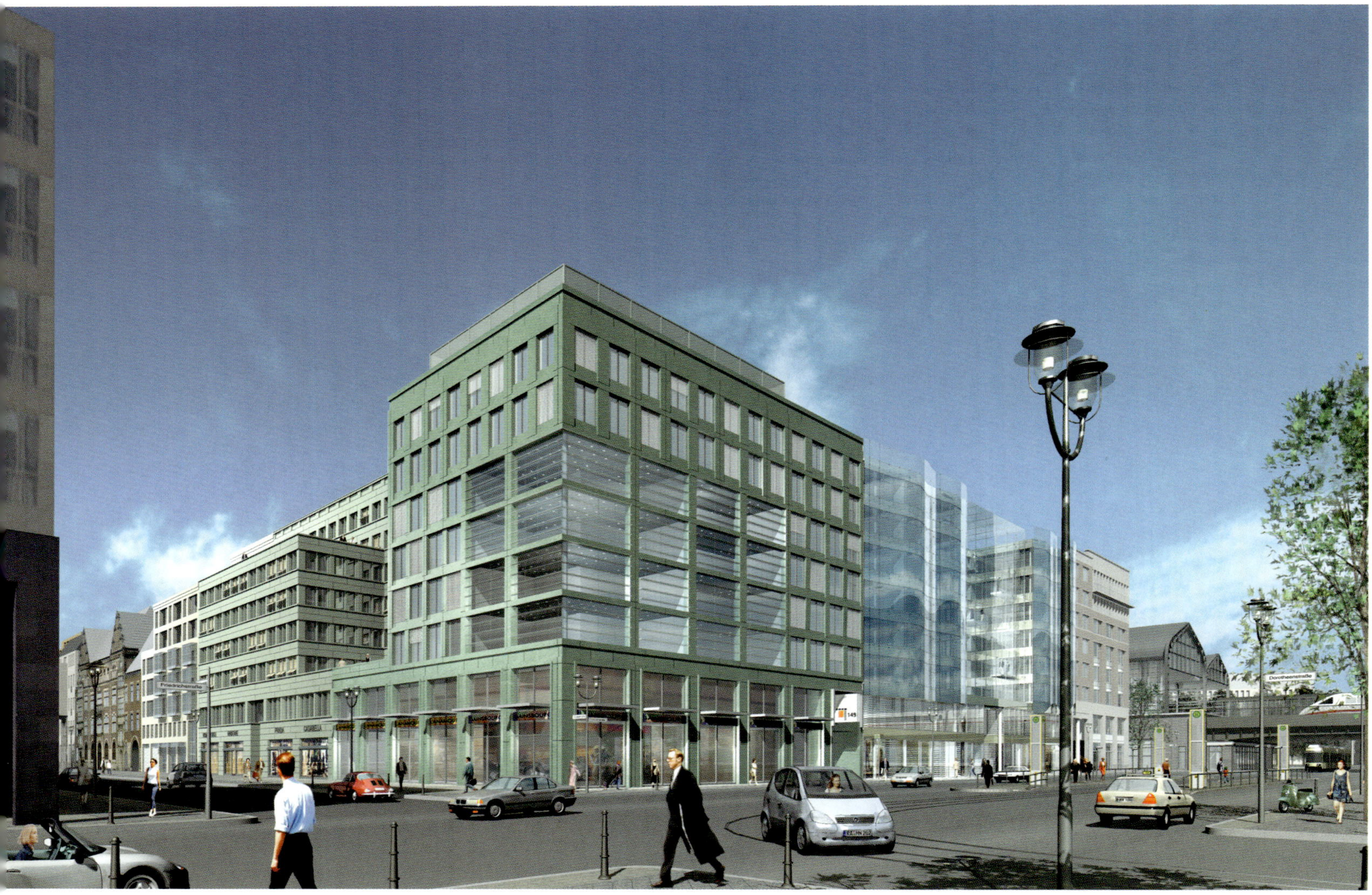

© Züblin, archimation

Friedrich Carré

Assmann Salomon und Partner,
Eike Becker Gesellschaft von Architekten GmbH,
Walter A. Noebel, Architekten Metz Klotz & Partner,
Thomas Müller Ivan Reimann

2000–2002
Friedrichstraße · Georgenstraße · Dorotheenstraße

Büro, Gewerbe, Wohnen
Office, business, residence
Oficinas, comercio, viviendas

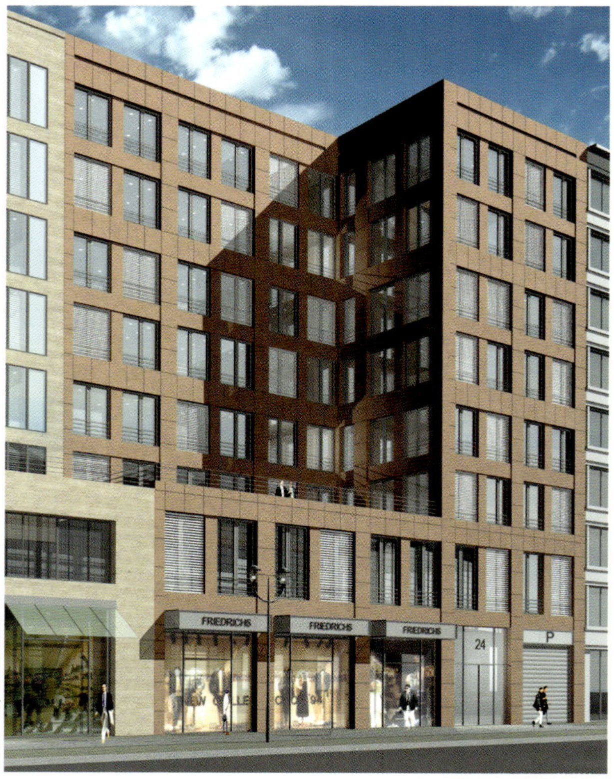

© Züblin, archimation

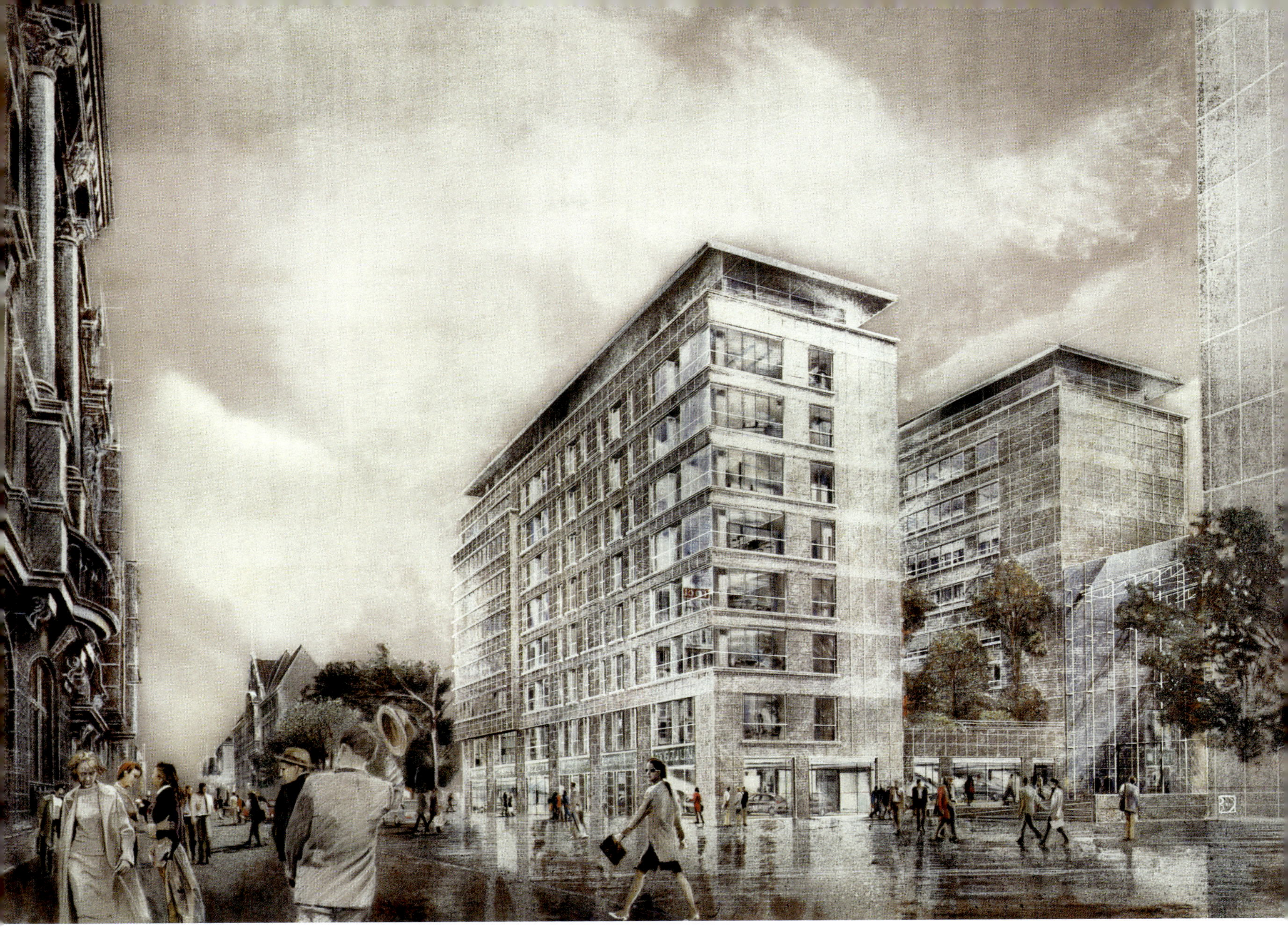

Neues Internationales Handelszentrum Berlin
RKW Rhode Kellermann Wawrowsky
Architektur + Städtebau, Berlin
2000–2002
Friedrichstraße
Büro, Gewerbe, Wohnen
Office, business, residence
Oficinas, comercio, viviendas

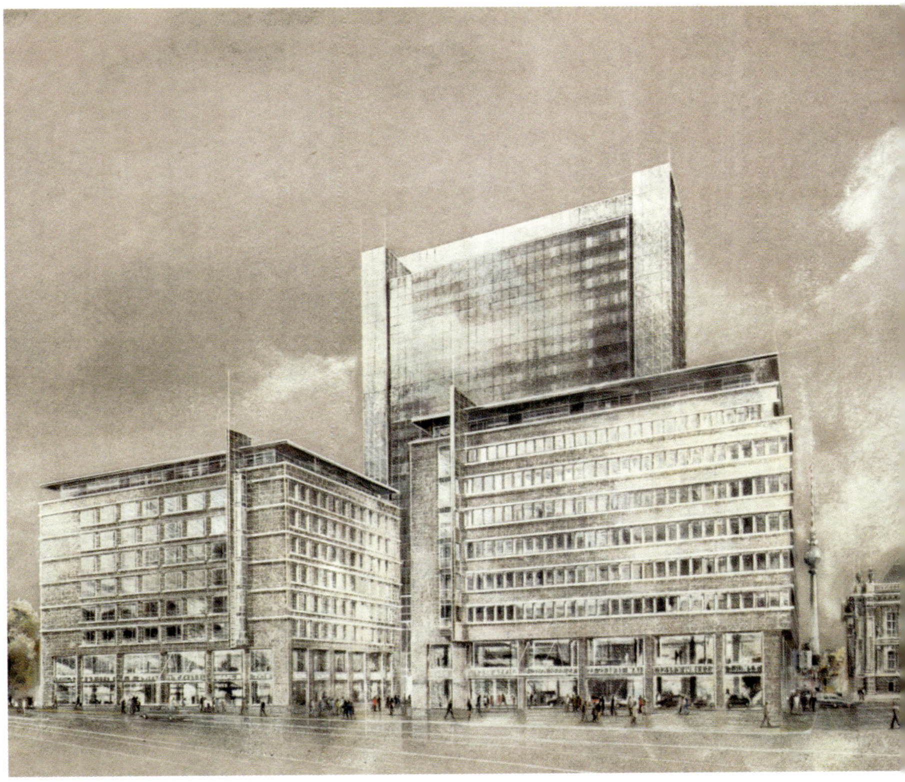

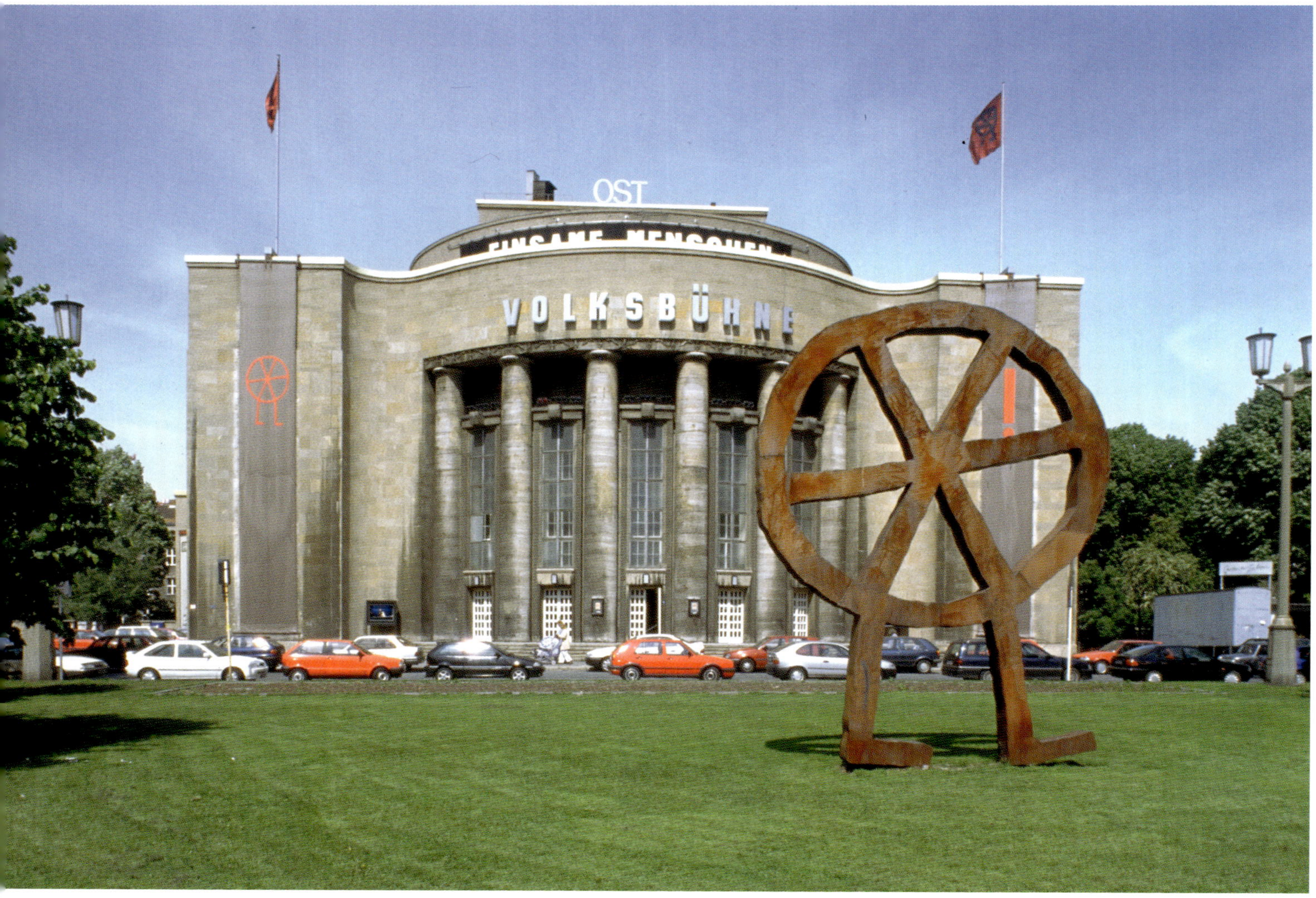

Volksbühne
Oskar Kaufmann,
Hans Richter
1913–1915,
1950–1954
Rosa-Luxemburg-Platz
Theater · theatre · teatro

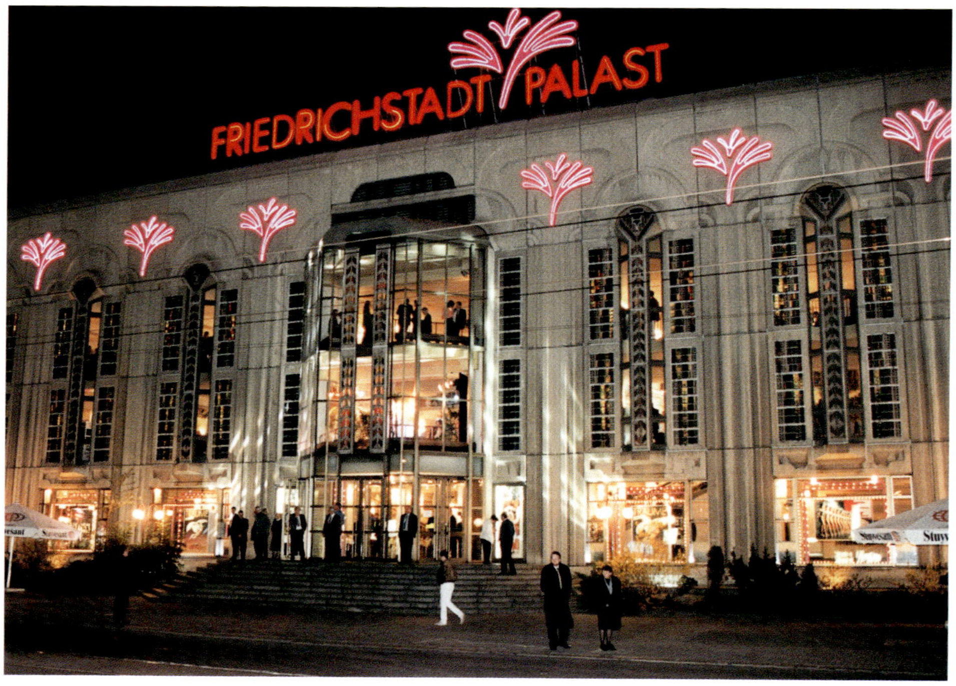

Friedrichstadtpalast
Walter Schwarz,
Manfred Prasser,
Dieter Bankert
1981–1984
Friedrichstraße
Theater · theatre · teatro

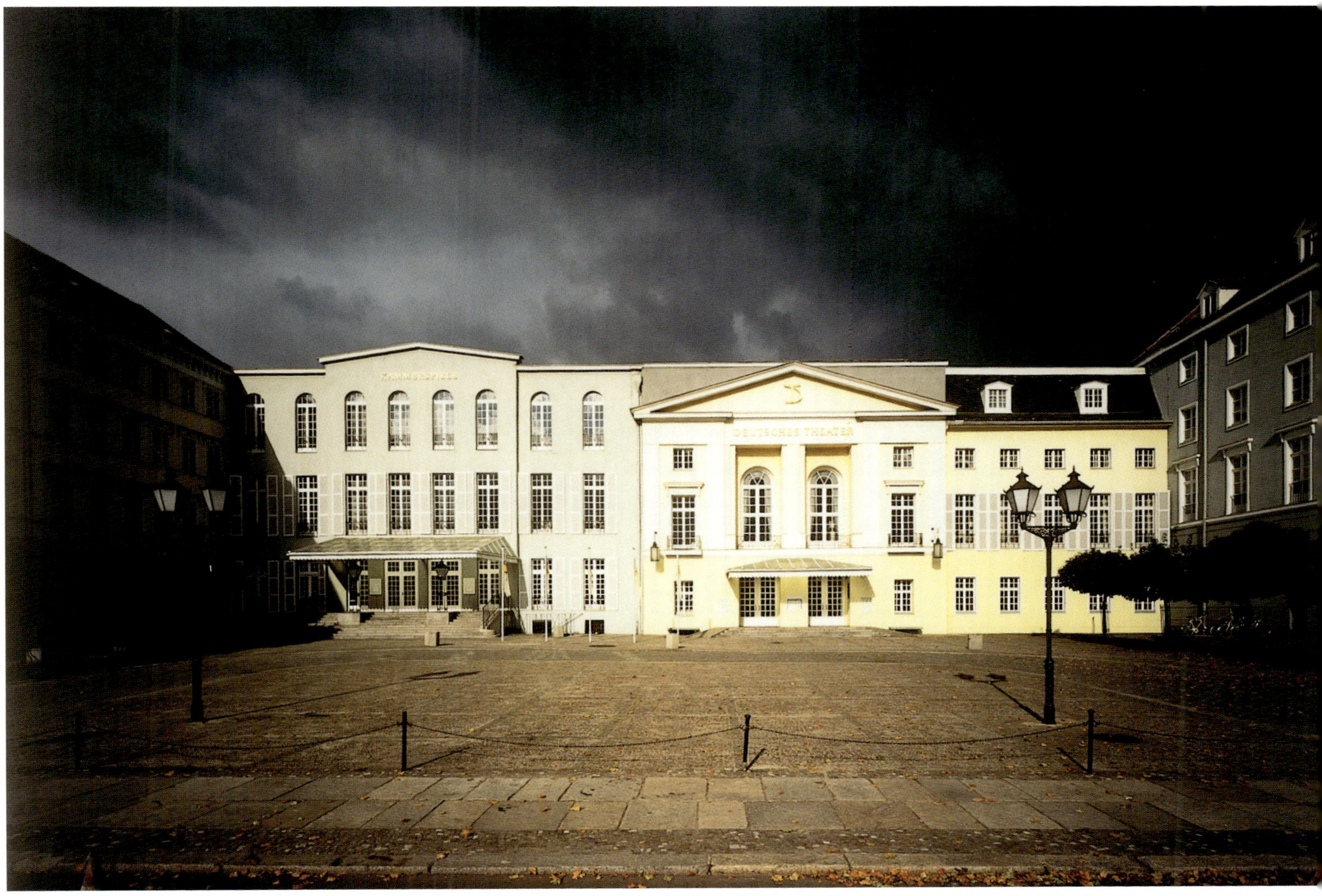

Deutsches Theater und Kammerspiele
Eduard Titz, Alfred Messel,
William Müller
1849–1850,
1905–1906
Schumannstraße
Theater · theatre · teatro

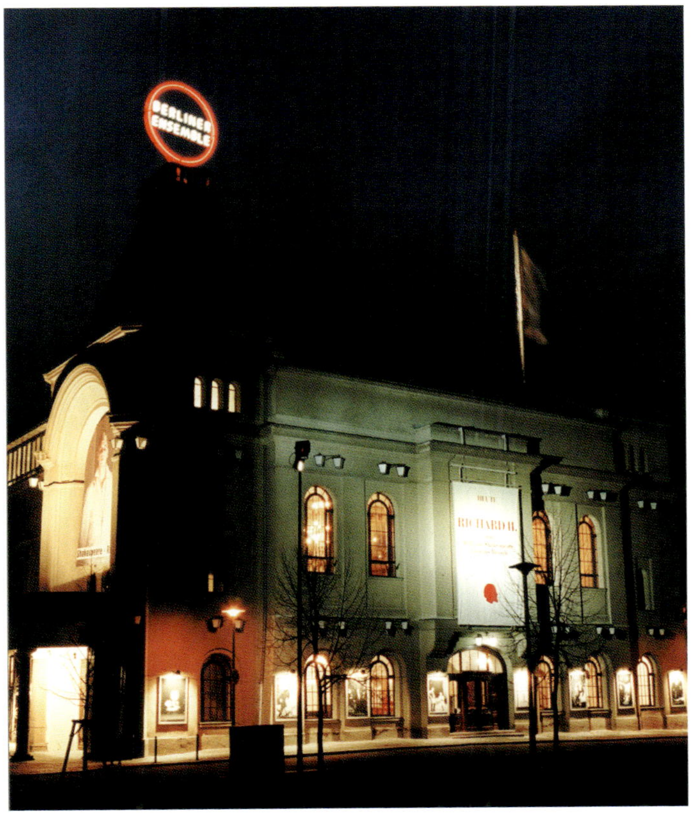

Berliner Ensemble
(ehemaliges Neues Theater
am Schiffbauerdamm)
Heinrich Seeling
1891–1892
Schiffbauerdamm
Theater · theatre · teatrc

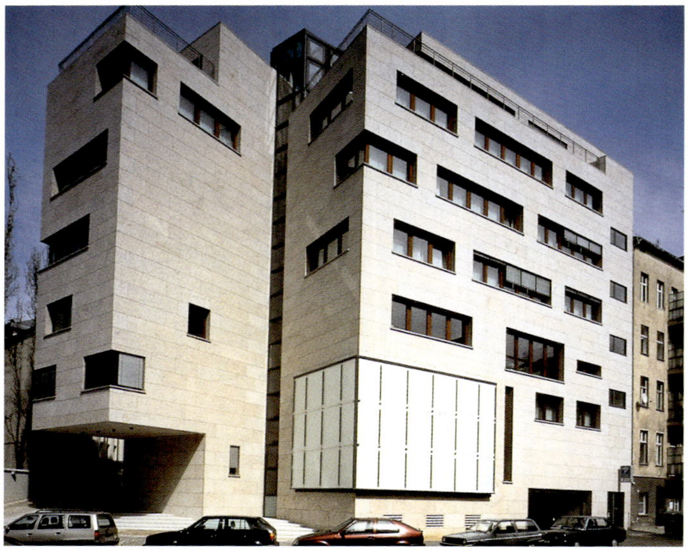

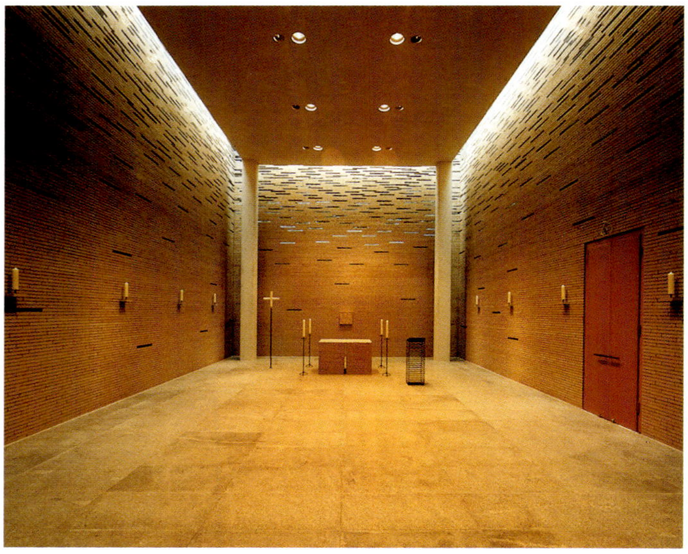

Deutsche Bischofskonferenz, Erweiterung Katholische Akademie
German Bishop's Conference, Extension for the Catholic Academy
Conferencia Episcopal Alemana, Amplición de la Academia Católica
Höger Hare Architekten, Berlin
1997–1999
Hannoversche Straße · Chausseestraße

Café Bravo
Nalbach + Nalbach, Berlin,
Konzeptkünstler · Concept artist ·
Artista conceptual: Dan Graham, New York
1998–1999
Auguststraße
Ausstellungsort, Gewerbe
Exhibition hall, business
Sala de exposiciones, comercio

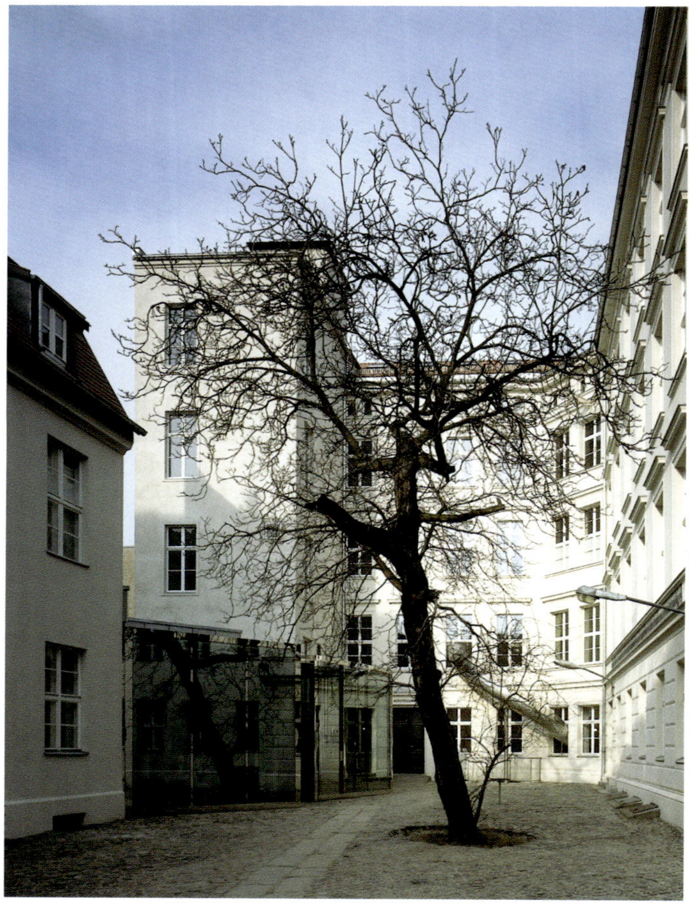

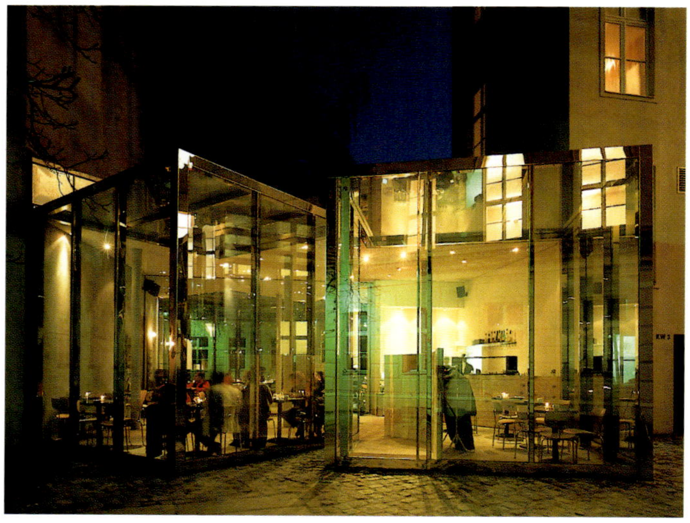

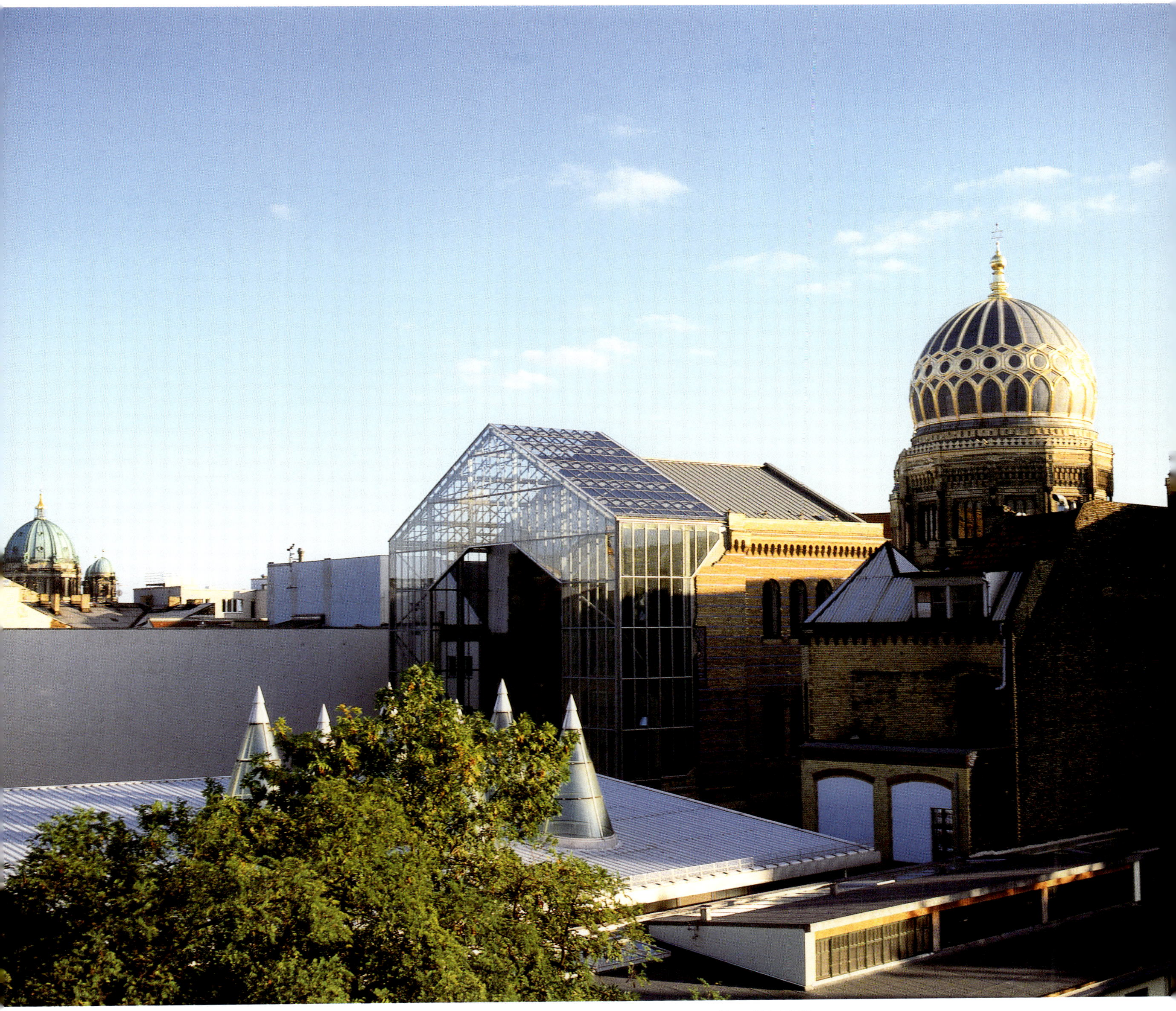

Neue Synagoge
EDUARD KNOBLAUCH, FRIEDRICH AUGUST STÜLER,
BERNHARD LEISERING, Berlin
1859–1866,
1989–1995
Oranienburger Straße
Synagoge, Kultur, Museum
Synagogue, culture, museum
Sinagoga, cultura, museo

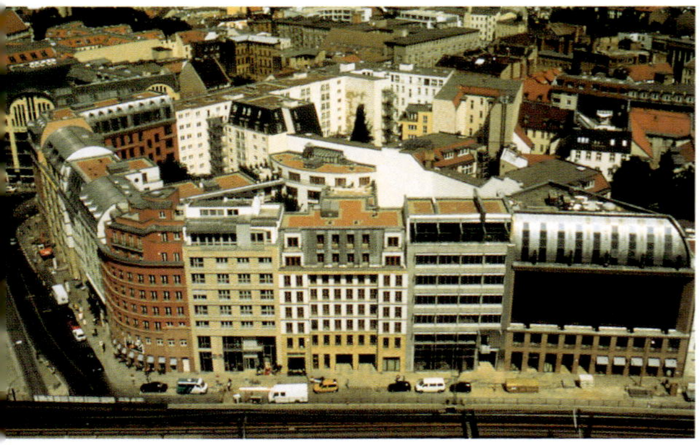

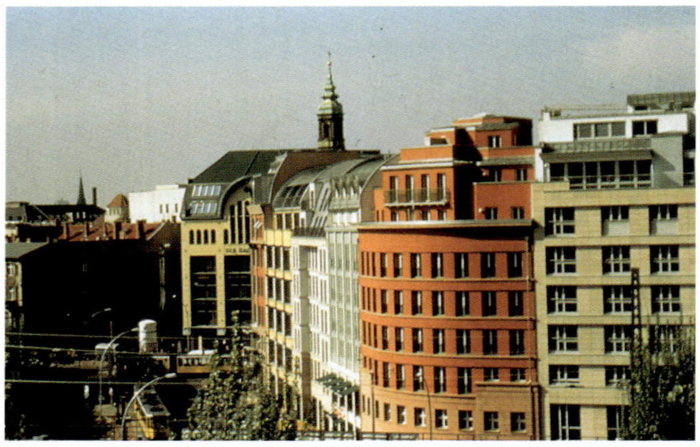

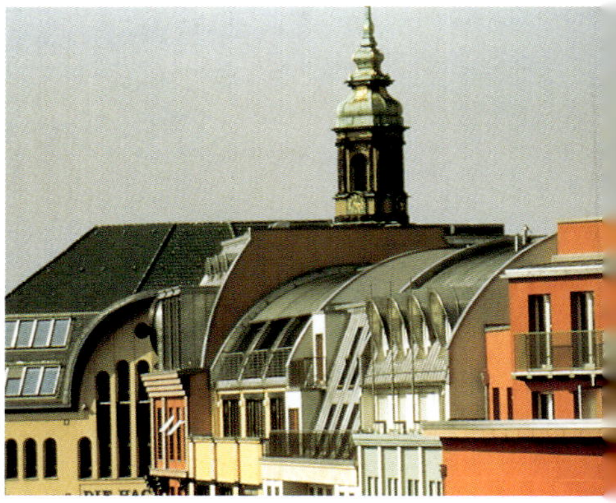

Neuer Hackescher Markt
Götz Bellmann & Walter Böhm, Berlin
1996–1998
Zwischen Dircksen- und Rosenthaler Straße
Büro, Gewerbe, Wohnen, Kultur
Office, business, residence, culture
Oficinas, comercio, viviendas, cultura

Hackesche Höfe
Kurt Berndt, August Endell, Weiss & Partner
1906–1907,
1995–1997
Rosenthaler Straße · Sophienstraße
Büro, Gewerbe, Wohnen, Kultur
Office, business, residence, culture
Oficinas, comercio, viviendas, cultura

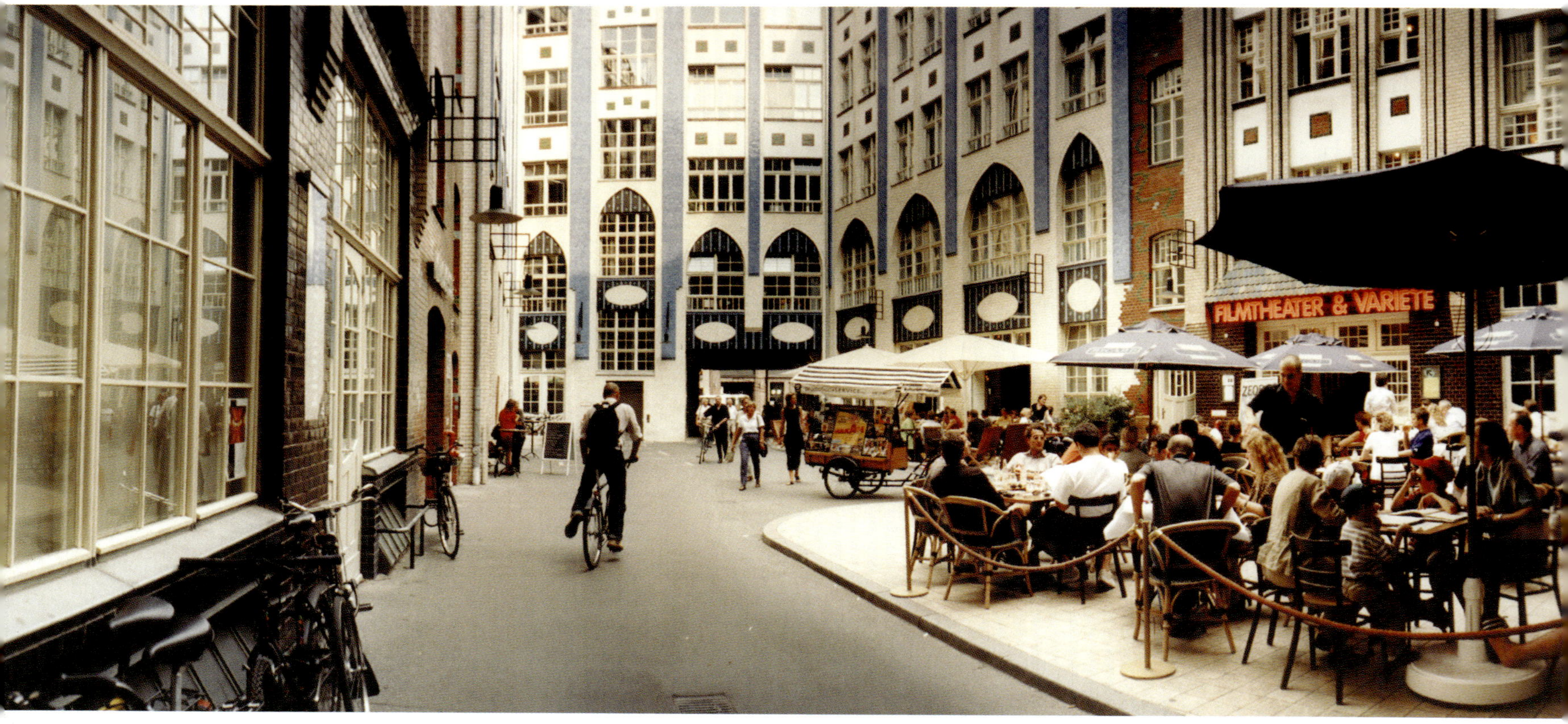

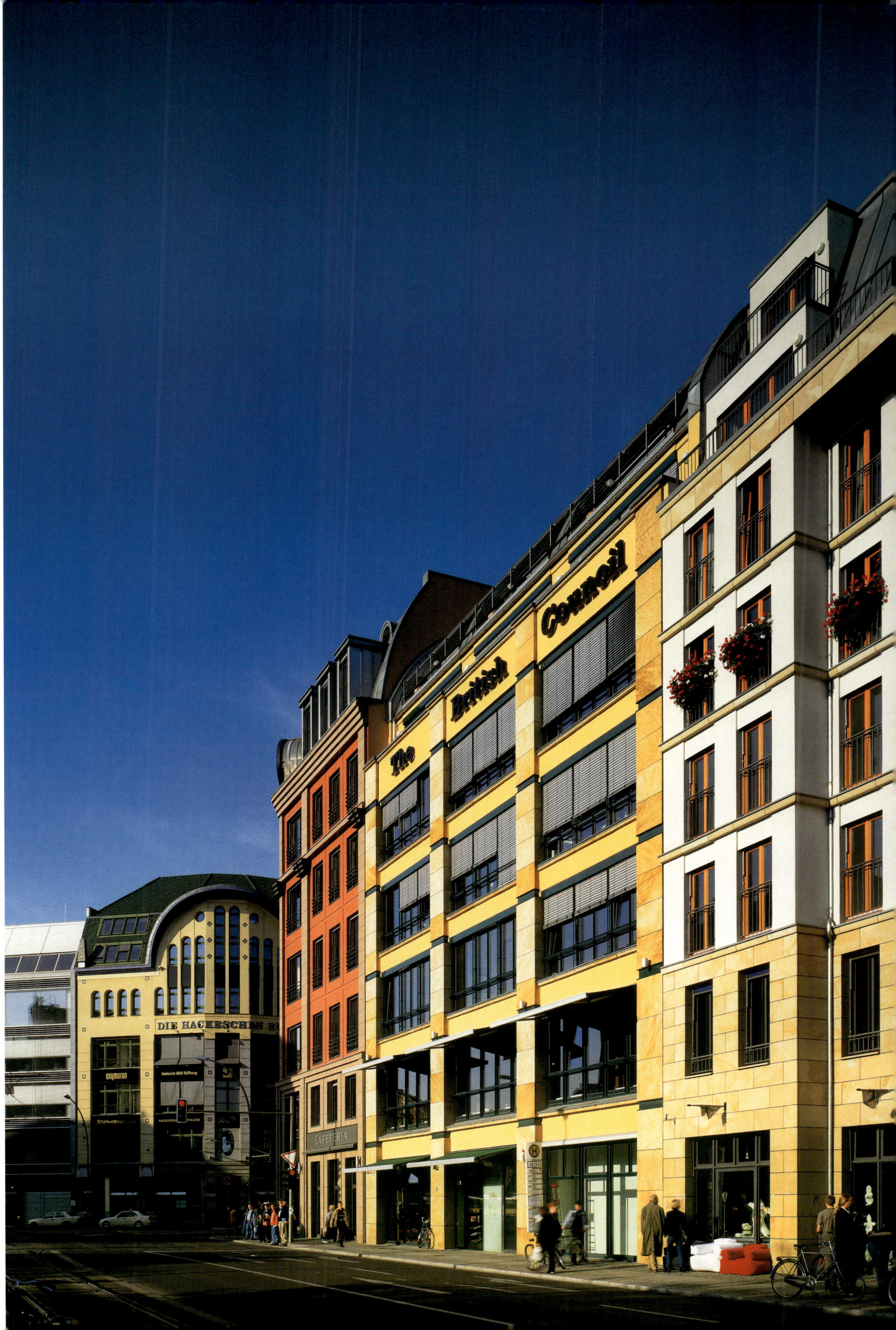
The British Council
DIE HACKESCHEN
oxymoron
CAFETERIA

Berliner Dom

Julius Carl Raschdorff,
Otto Raschdorff,
Günther Stahn,
Bernhard Leisering

1884–1905,
1975–1993
Lustgarten

Kirche, Museum
Church, museum
Iglesia, museo

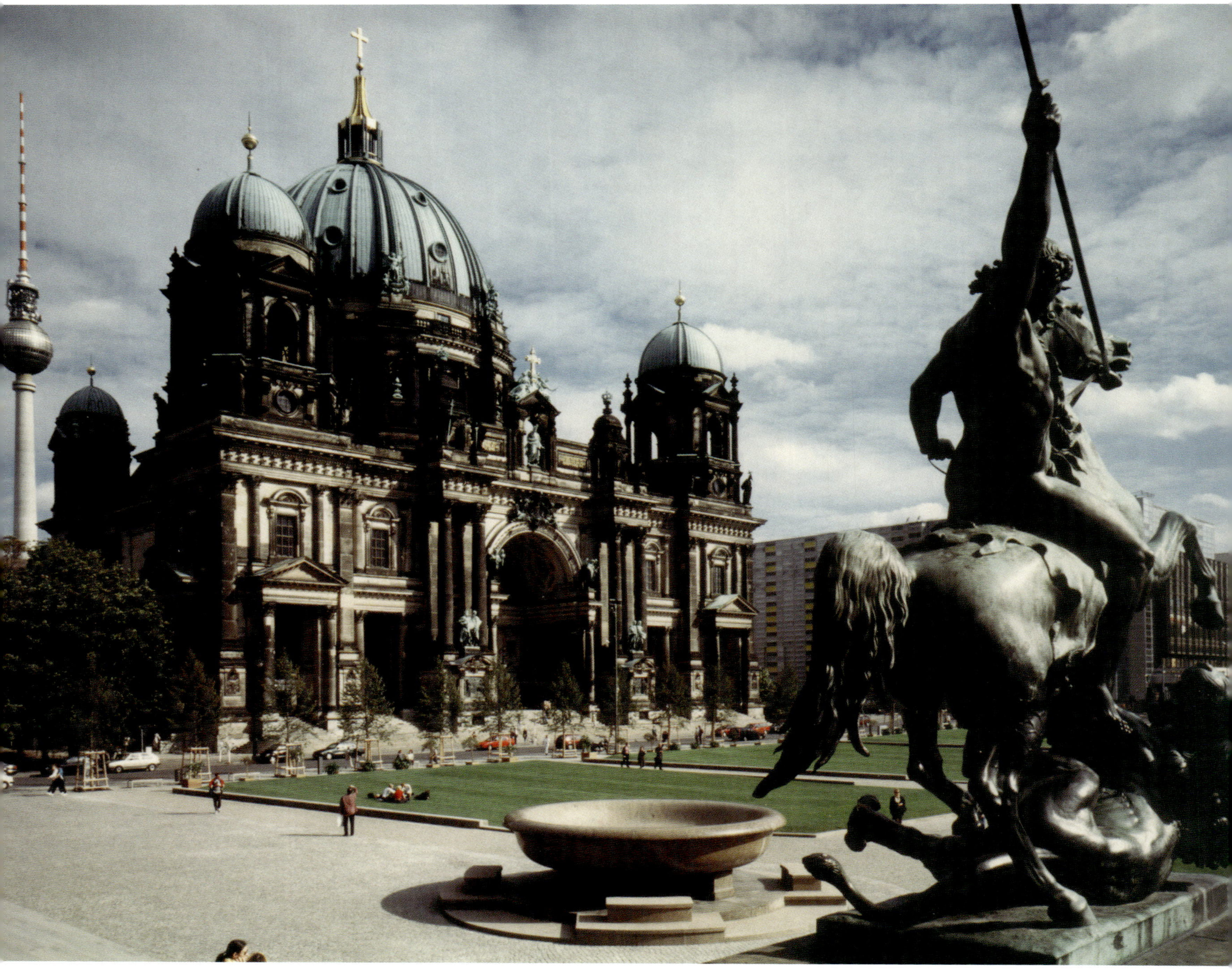

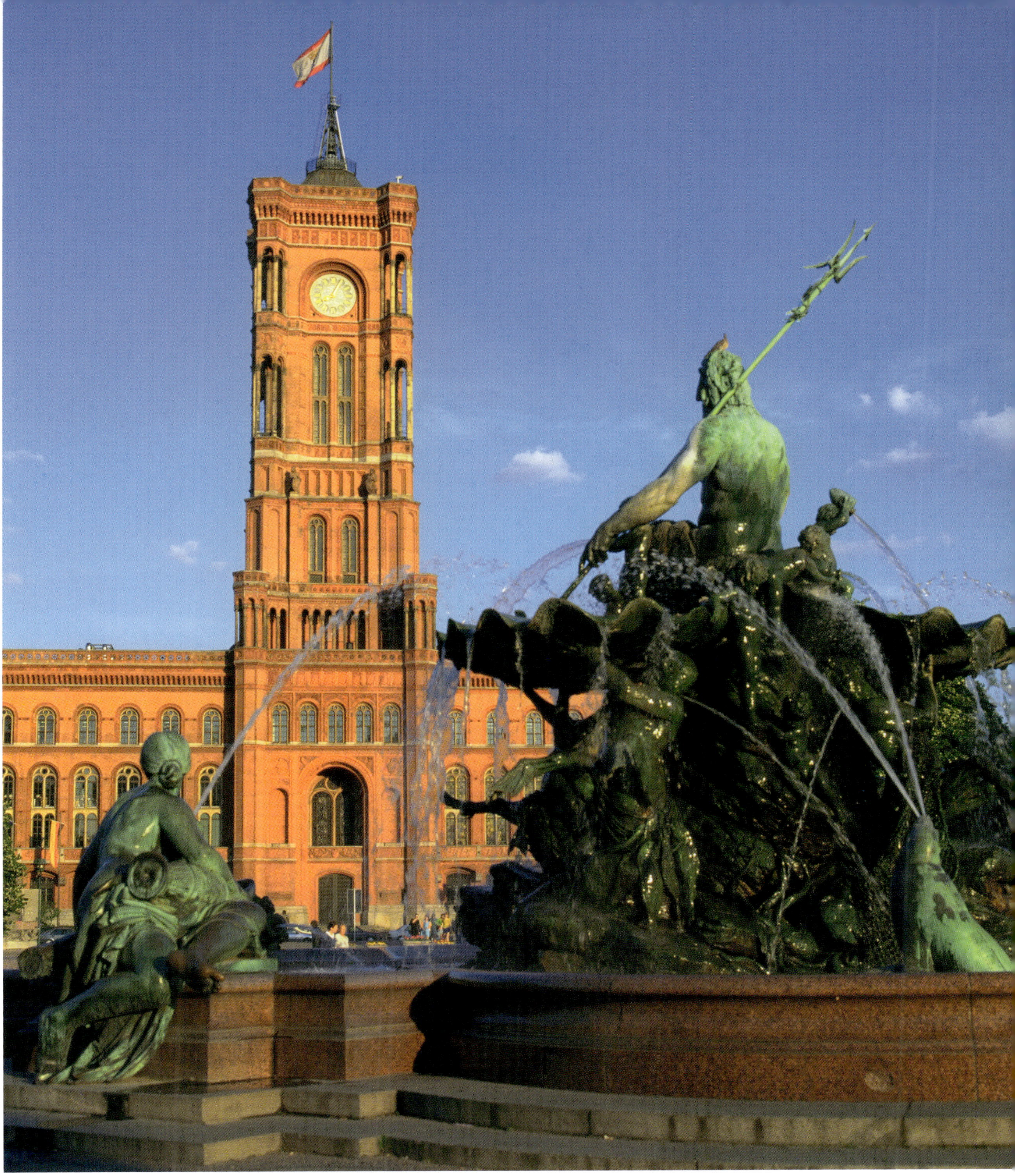

Berliner Rathaus · **Berlin Town Hall** · **Ayuntamiento de Berlín**
Herrmann Friedrich Waesemann
1861–1869
Rathausstraße
Senatskanzlei · Senate Chancellery · Cancillería del Gobierno Municipal

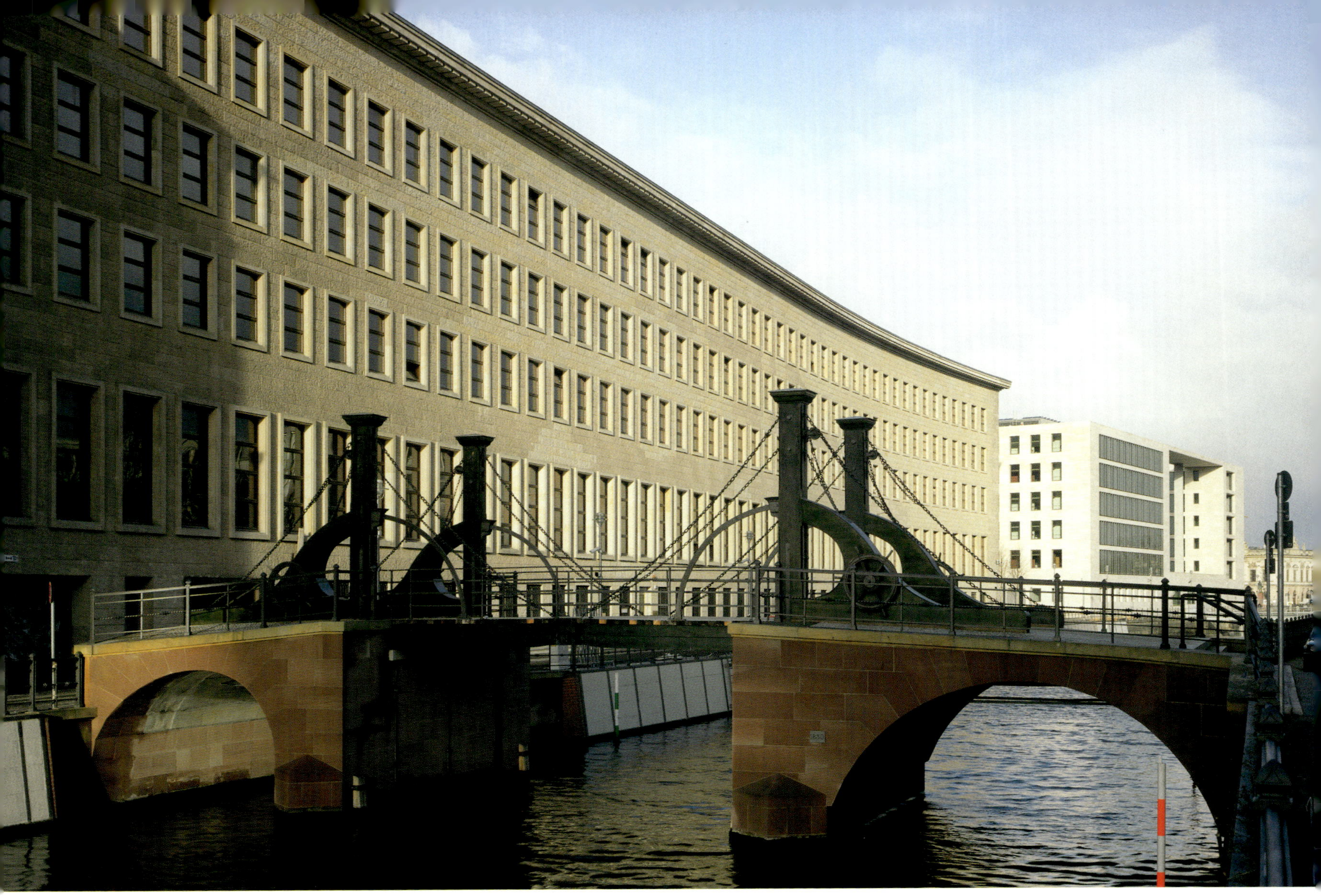

Auswärtiges Amt · Altbau (ehemals Reichsbank) und Neubau
The Foreign Ministry · old building (former Reichsbank) and new building
Ministerio de Asuntos Exteriores · edificio original (antiguo Banco del Reich) y reforma
Heinrich Wolff (Altbau · old building · edificio original),
Hans Kollhoff, Berlin (Umbau Altbau · alteration · reforma),
Müller Reimann Architekten, Berlin (Neubau · new building · construcción nueva)
1939, 1997–1999
Werderscher Markt

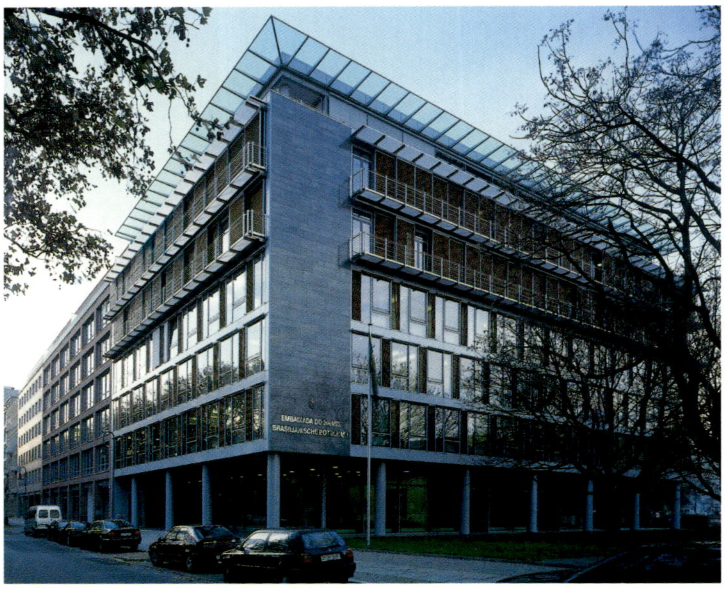

Botschaft der Föderativen Republik Brasilien
Embassy of Brasil
Embajada de la República Federal de Brasil
PSP Pysall, Stahrenberg & Partner, Berlin
1998–2000
Wallstraße · Märkisches Ufer

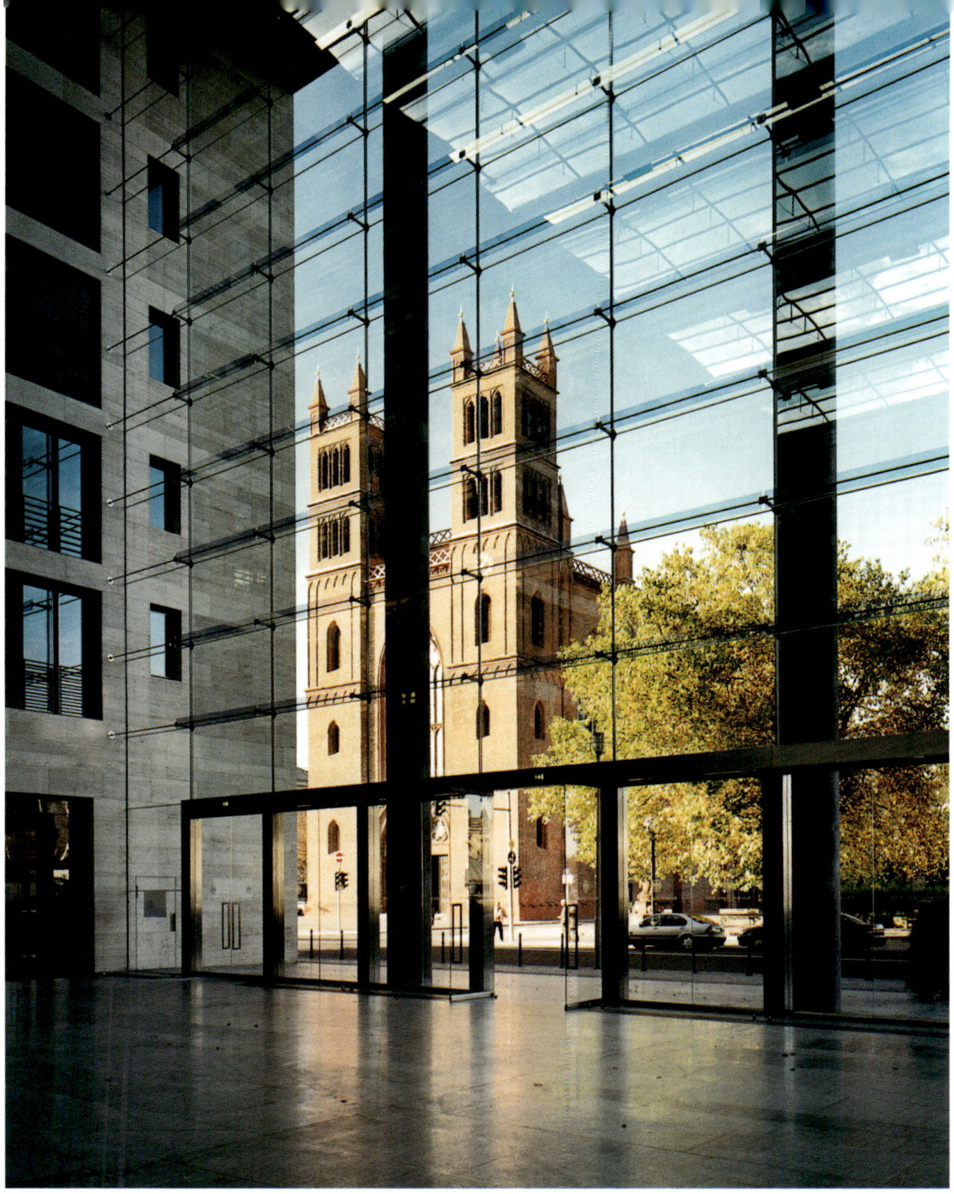

Blick aus dem Neubau des Auswärtigen Amtes und auf die Friedrichswerdersche Kirche
View out of the new building of the Foreign Ministry onto the Friedrichswerdersche Kirche
Iglesia de Friedrichswerder vista de la parte nueva del Ministerio de Asuntos Exteriores
Karl Friedrich Schinkel
1824–1830
Werderstraße
Museum · museum · museo

Falkoniergasse an der Friedrichswerderschen Kirche
Graetz Nöfer Tyrra,
Architektengesellschaft Friedrichswerder, Berlin
2001–2003
Oberwallstraße
Wohnen, Gewerbe
Residence, business
Viviendas, comercio

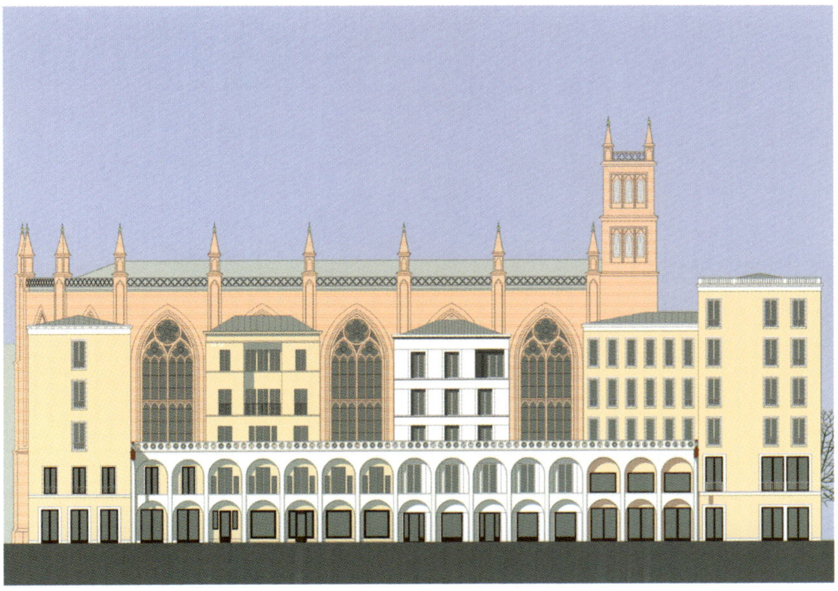

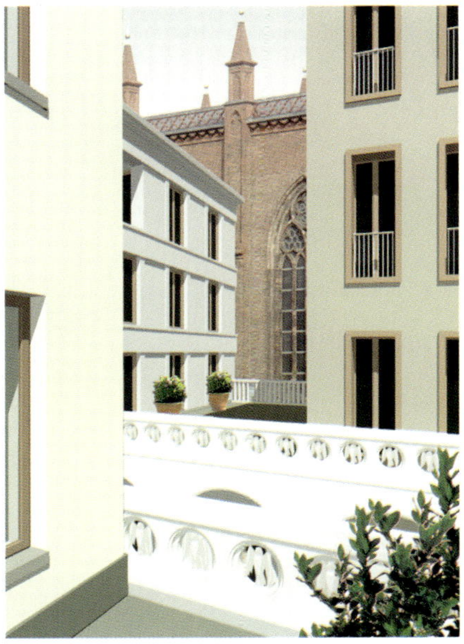

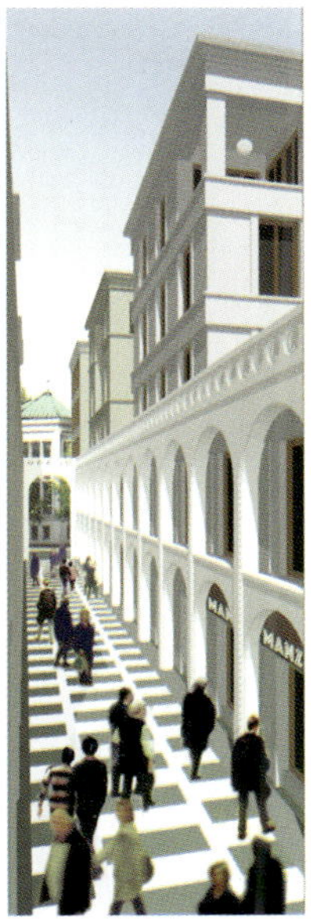

Nikolaiviertel mit Kirche St. Nikolai
um 1230
Nikolaikirchplatz
Kirche · church · iglesia

Ephraimpalais
Friedrich Wilhelm Diterichs
1762–1766,
1985–1987
(Rekonstruktion · reconstruction · reconstrucción)
Poststraße · Mühlendamm
Museum · museum · museo

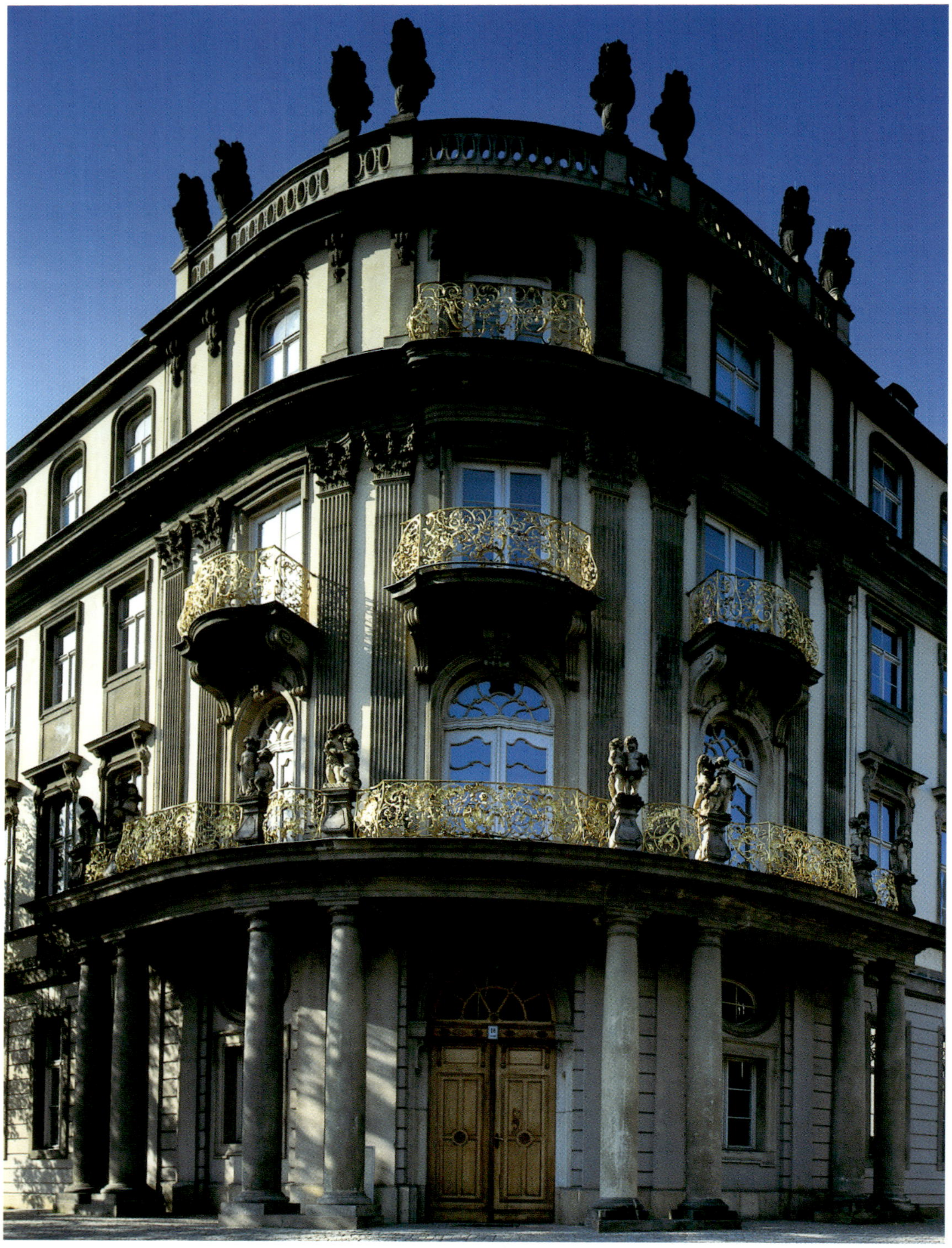

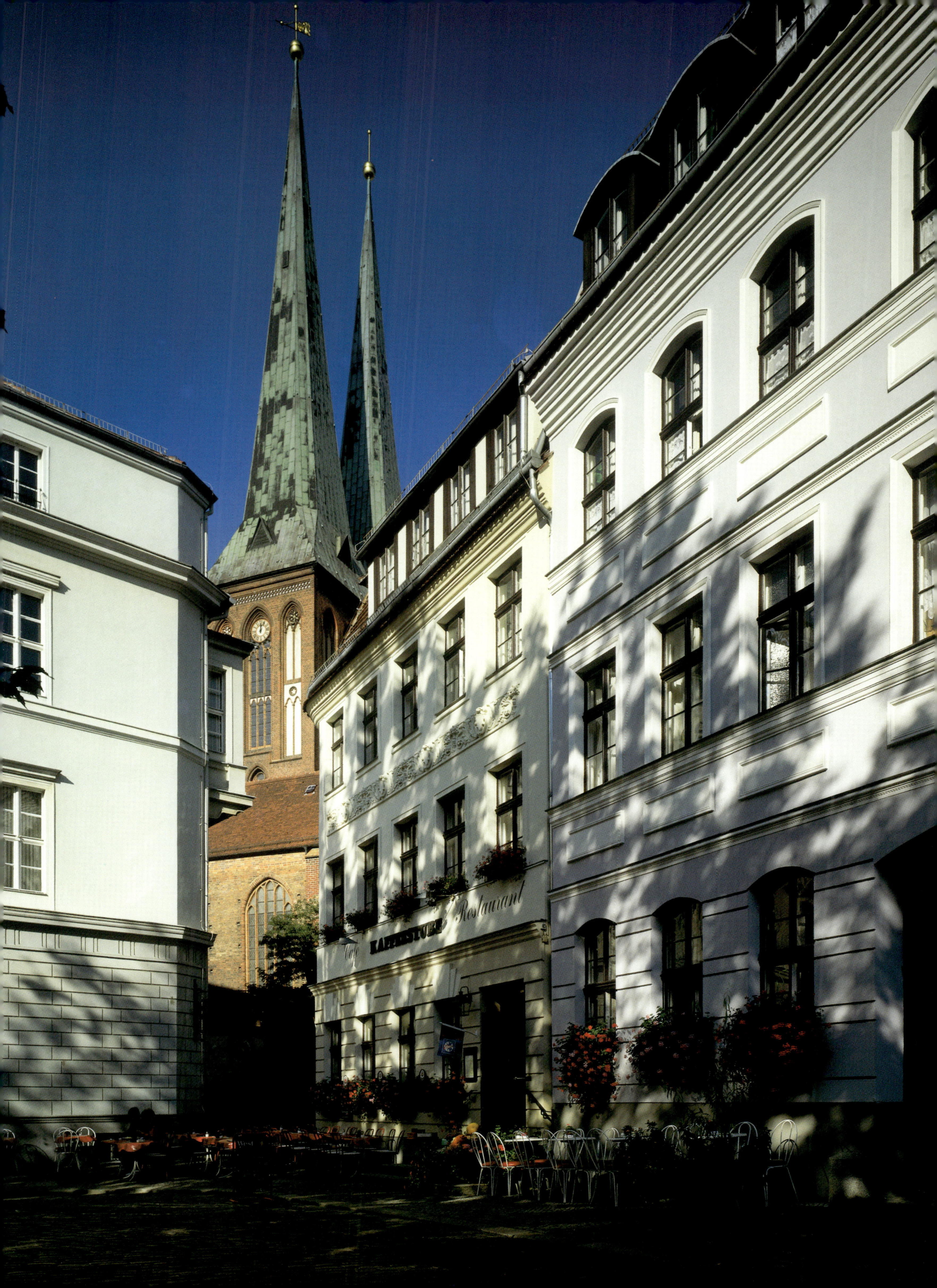
Cafe
KAFFEESTUBE
Restaurant

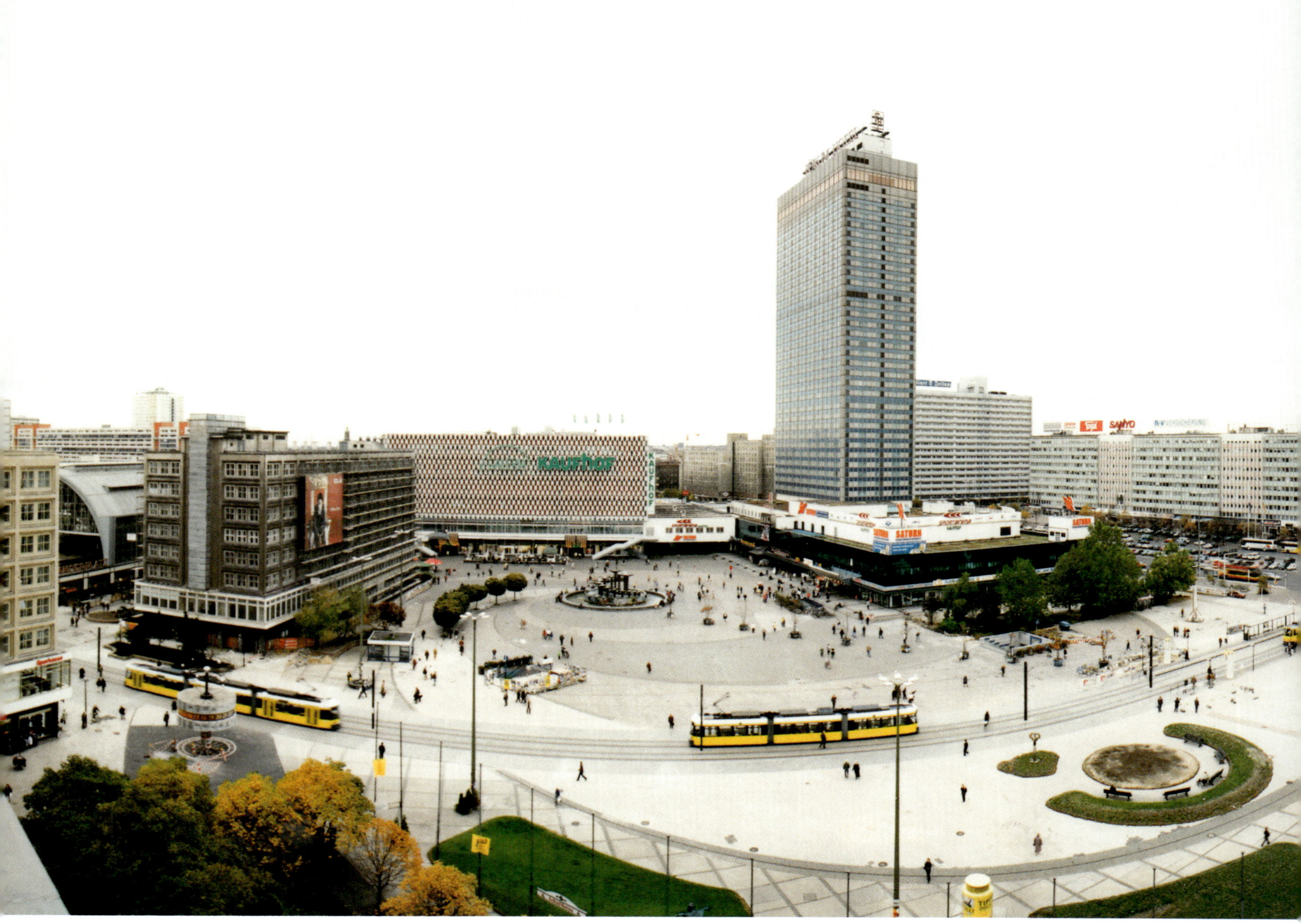

Gesamtansicht Alexanderplatz
Overview of Alexanderplatz
Panorama de Alexanderplatz
Von links nach rechts · from left to right · de izquierda a derecha: Alexanderhaus, Berolinahaus und Forum Hotel (ehemaliges · former · antiguo Hotel »Stadt Berlin«)
Peter Behrens, PSP Pysall, Stahrenberg & Partner, Berlin (Umbau und Restaurierung · rebuilding and restoration · reforma y restauración Alexander- und Berolinahaus), Heinz Scharlipp, Hans Erich Bogatzky (Forum Hotel)
1928–1932, 1992–1995 (Alexander- und Berolinahaus), 1967–1970 (Forum Hotel)
Büro, Gewerbe · office, business · oficina, comercio (Alexander- und Berolinahaus), Hotel · hotel · hotel (Forum Hotel)

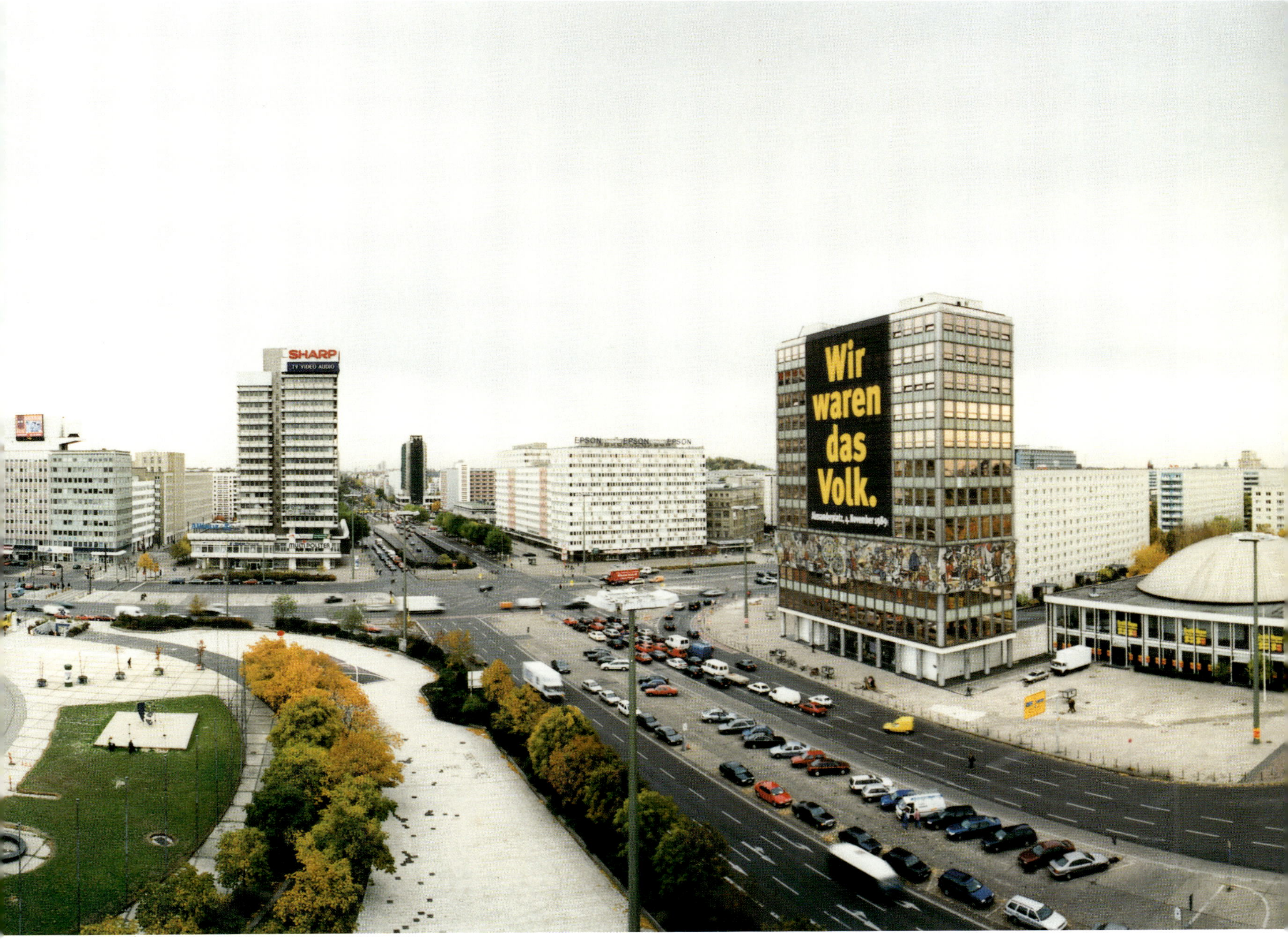
SHARP
TV VIDEO AUDIO
EPSON EPSON EPSON
Wir waren das Volk.

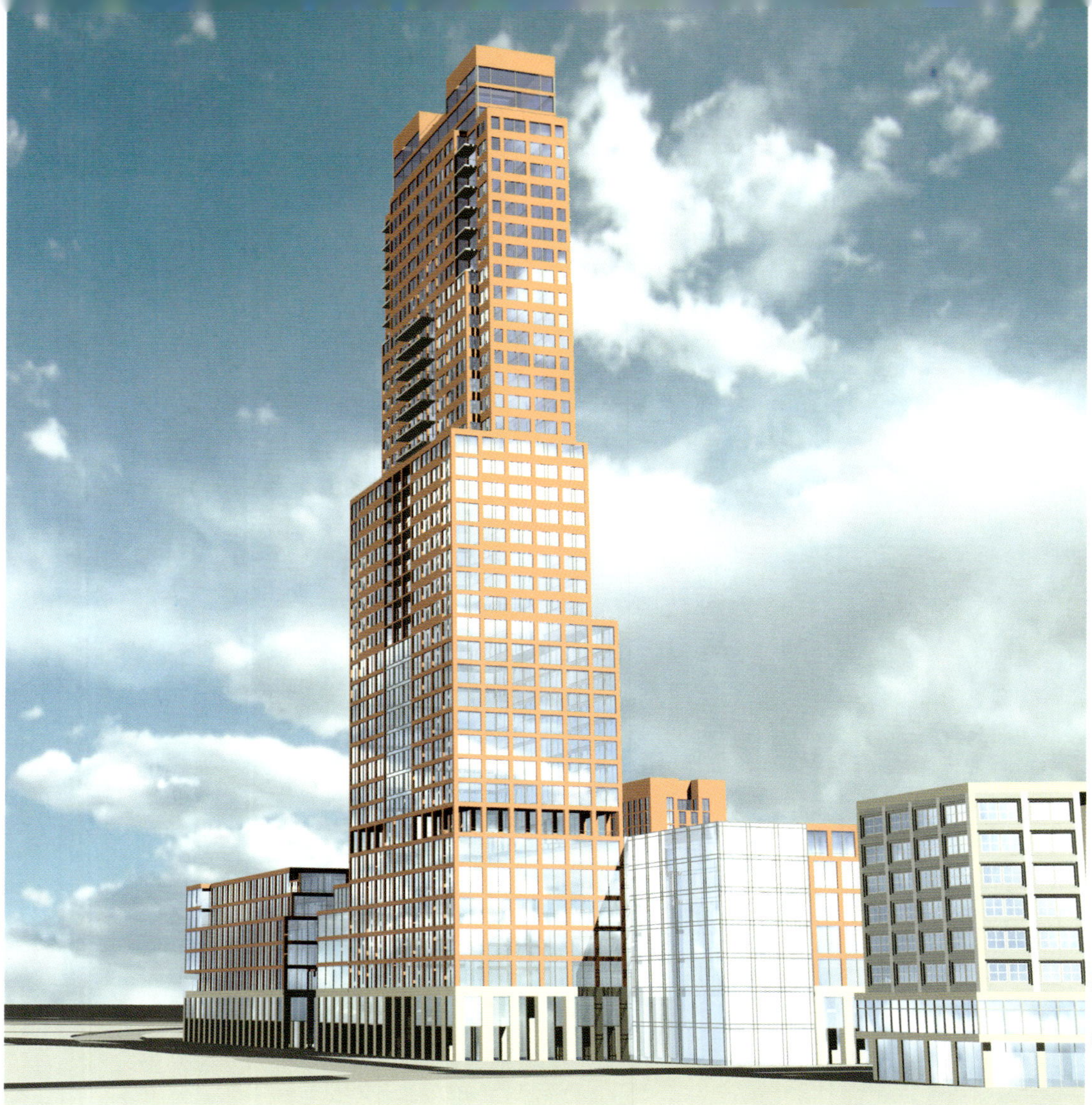

DEGEWO-Turm
Architekten N.N.,
Massestudie des
Architekturbüros
Kny & Weber, Berlin
geplant 2002–2006
Alexanderstraße ·
Gruner Straße
Büro, Gewerbe,
Wohnen, Hotel
Office, commerce,
residence, hotel
Oficina, comercio,
viviendas, hotel

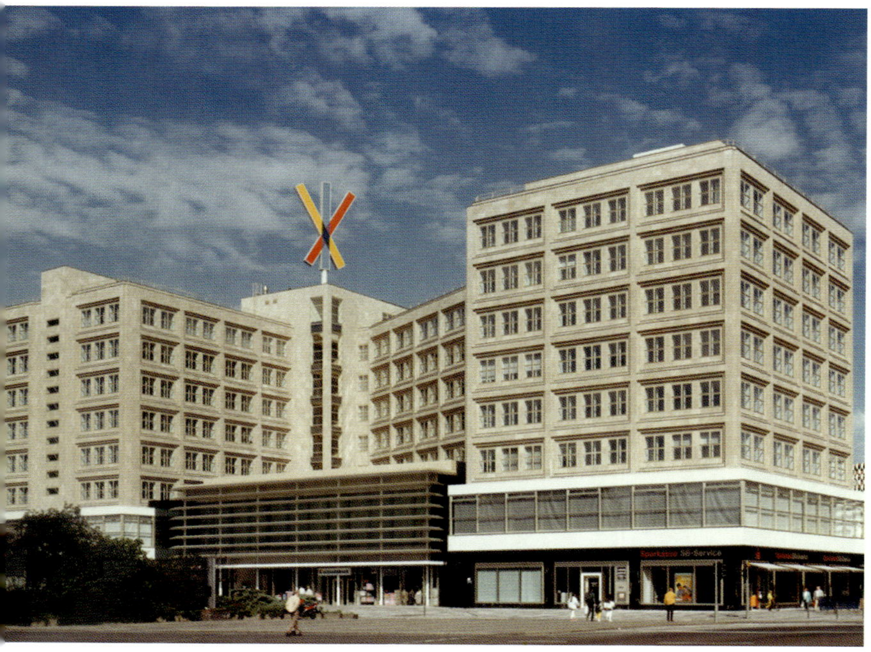

Alexanderhaus
Peter Behrens,
PSP Pysall, Stahrenberg
& Partner, Berlin
(Umbau und Restaurierung ·
rebuilding and restoration ·
reforma y restauración)
1928–1932,
1992–1995
Alexanderplatz
Büro, Gewerbe
Office, business
Oficina, comercio

Ehemaliges Preußisches Abgeordnetenhaus
Former Prussian House of Representatives
Antiguo Parlamento de Prusia
Friedrich Schulze-Colditz
1892–1897
Niederkirchnerstraße
Sitz des Berliner Abgeordnetenhauses
Seat of the Berlin House of Representatives
Sede del Parlamento de Berlín

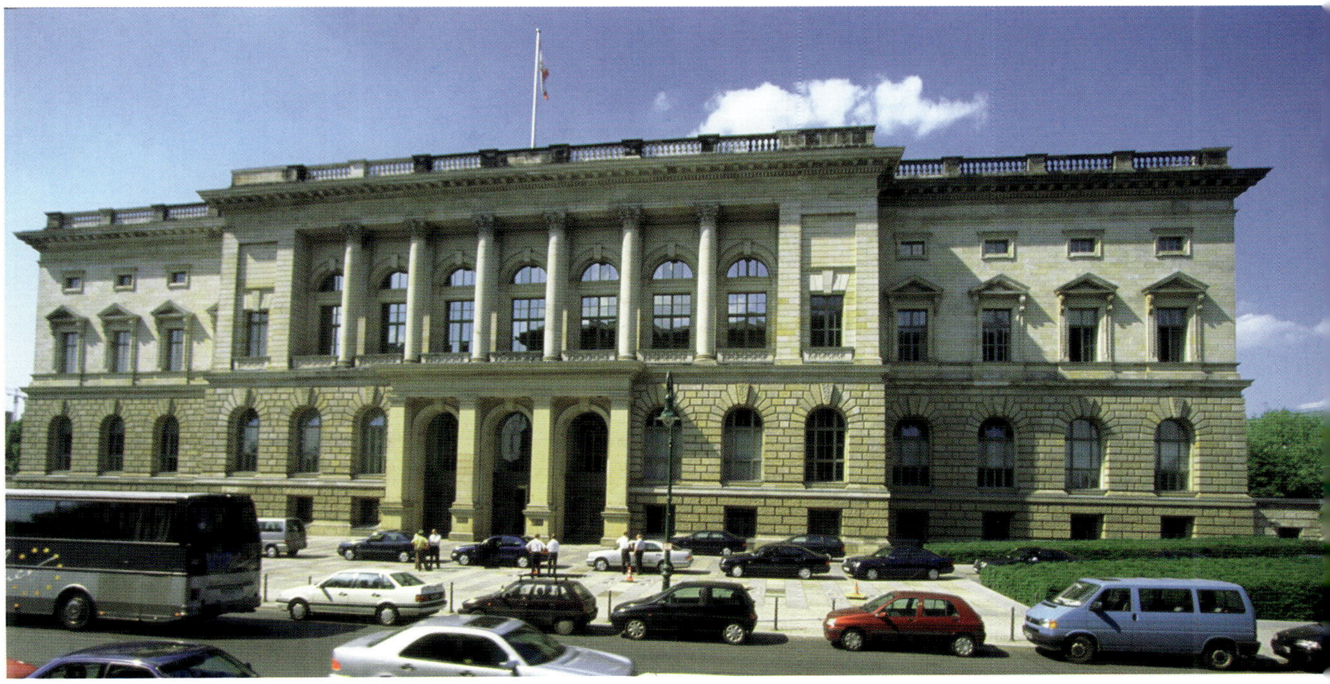

Martin-Gropius-Bau
Martin Gropius, Heino Schmieden
1877–1881
Stresemannstraße
Ausstellungsort
Exhibition hall
Centro de exposiciones

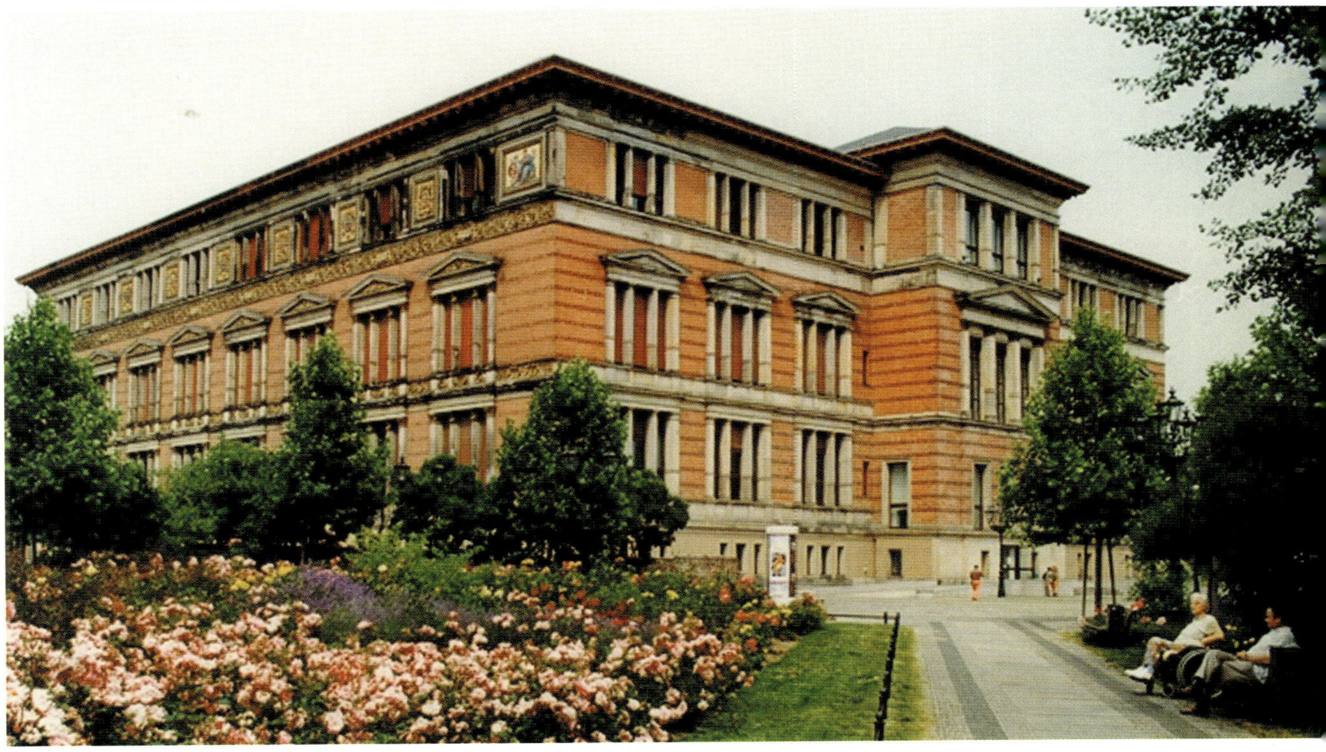

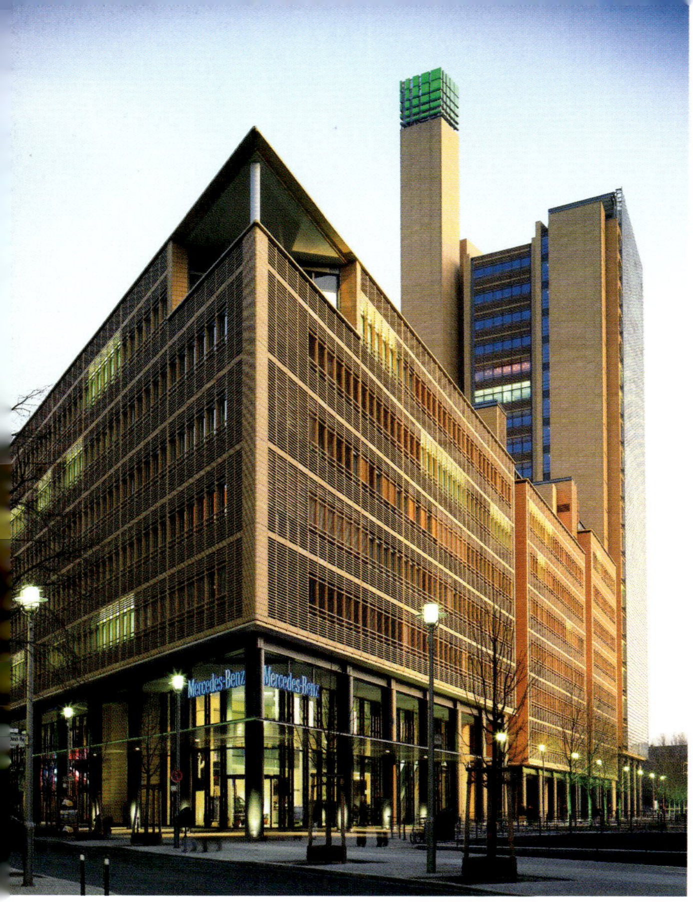

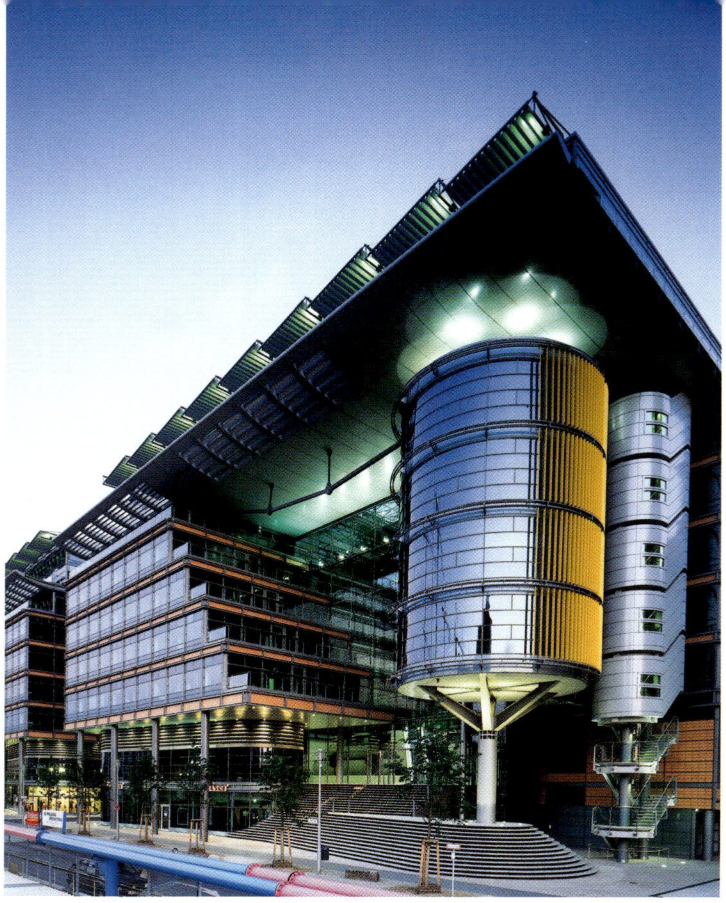

Headquarters DaimlerChrysler Services AG
Renzo Piano, Paris
1996–1998
Eichhornstraße
Büro, Gewerbe, Wohnen
Office, business, residence
Oficinas, comercio, viviendas

Büro-, Wohn- und Geschäftshäuser Potsdamer Platz
Richard Rogers Partnership, London
1996–1998
Linkstraße
Büro, Gewerbe, Wohnen
Office, business, residence
Oficinas, comercio, viviendas

Musical-Theater
Renzo Piano, Paris
1996–1998
Marlene-Dietrich-Platz
Theater · theatre · teatro

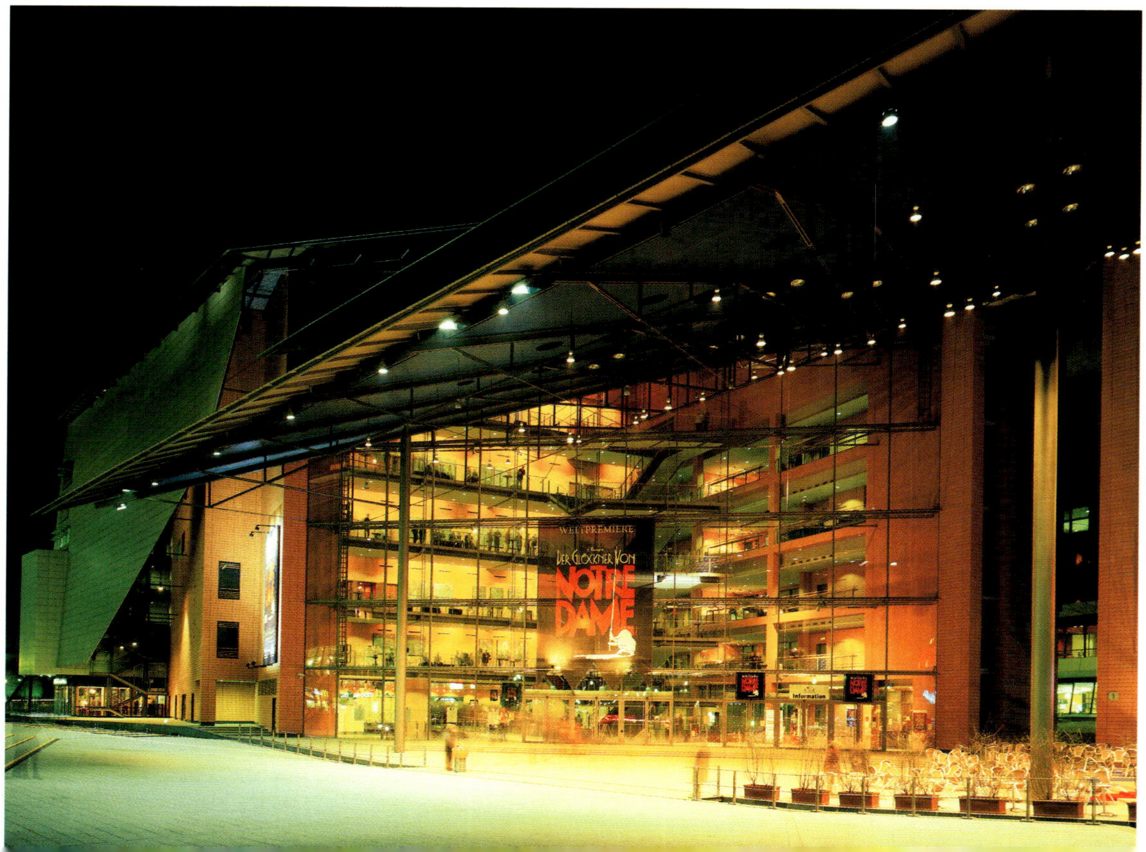

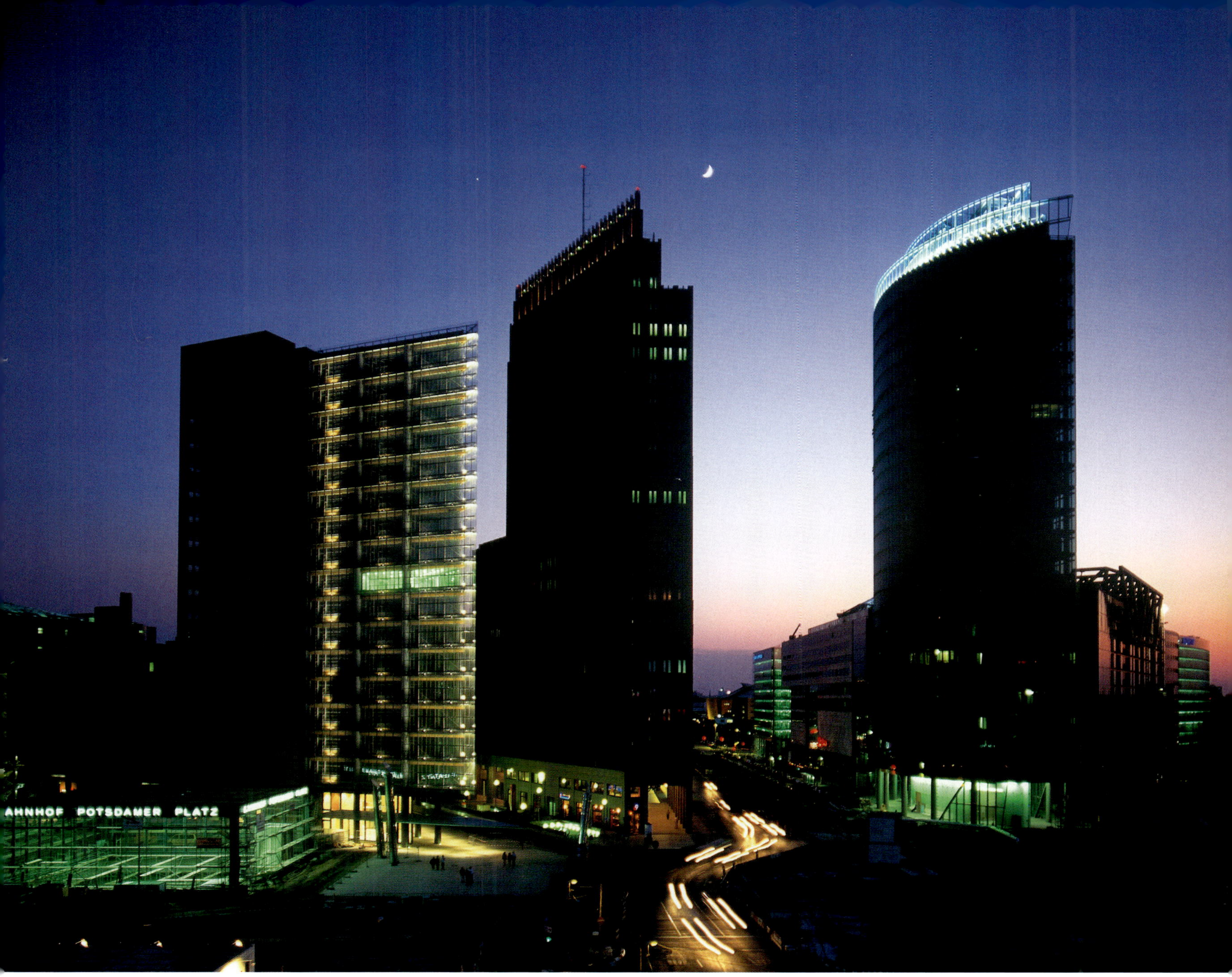

Ansicht Potsdamer Platz von Osten
View of Potsdamer Platz from the east
Panorama de la Potsdamer Platz desde el este
Von links nach rechts · from left to right · de izquierda a derecha: Büro- und Geschäftshäuser, Sony Center
Renzo Piano, Paris, Kollhoff & Timmermann, Berlin, Murphy/Jahn Architects, Chicago
1996–1999, 1995–1999, 1996–2000
Alte Potsdamer Straße, Potsdamer Straße
Büro, Gewerbe, Wohnen
Office, business, residence
Oficinas, comercio, viviendas

Bahnhof Potsdamer Platz
Architektengemeinschaft Hilmer + Sattler, München/Berlin, Modersohn & Freiesleben, Berlin
1997–2000

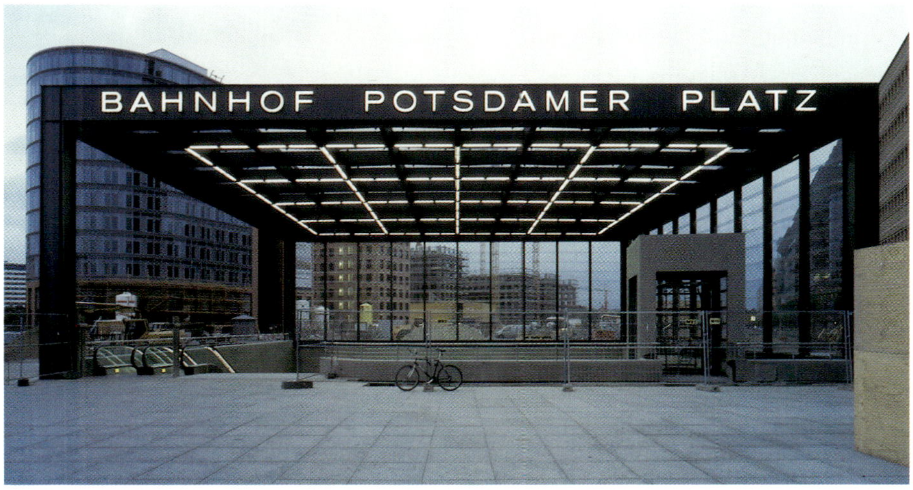

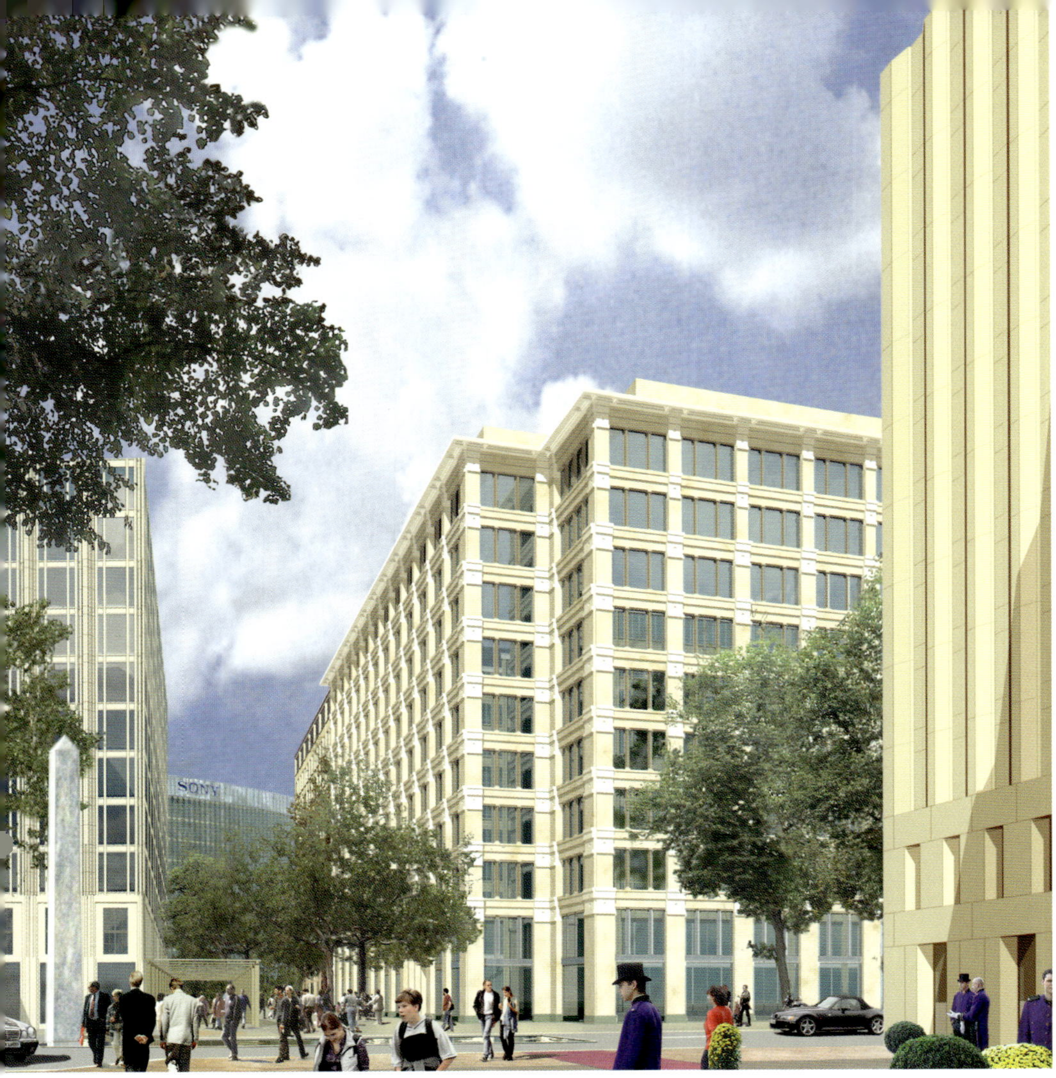

Bürohaus
Hilmer + Sattler + Albrecht, Berlin
2001–2003
Potsdamer Platz
Gewerbe · business · comercio

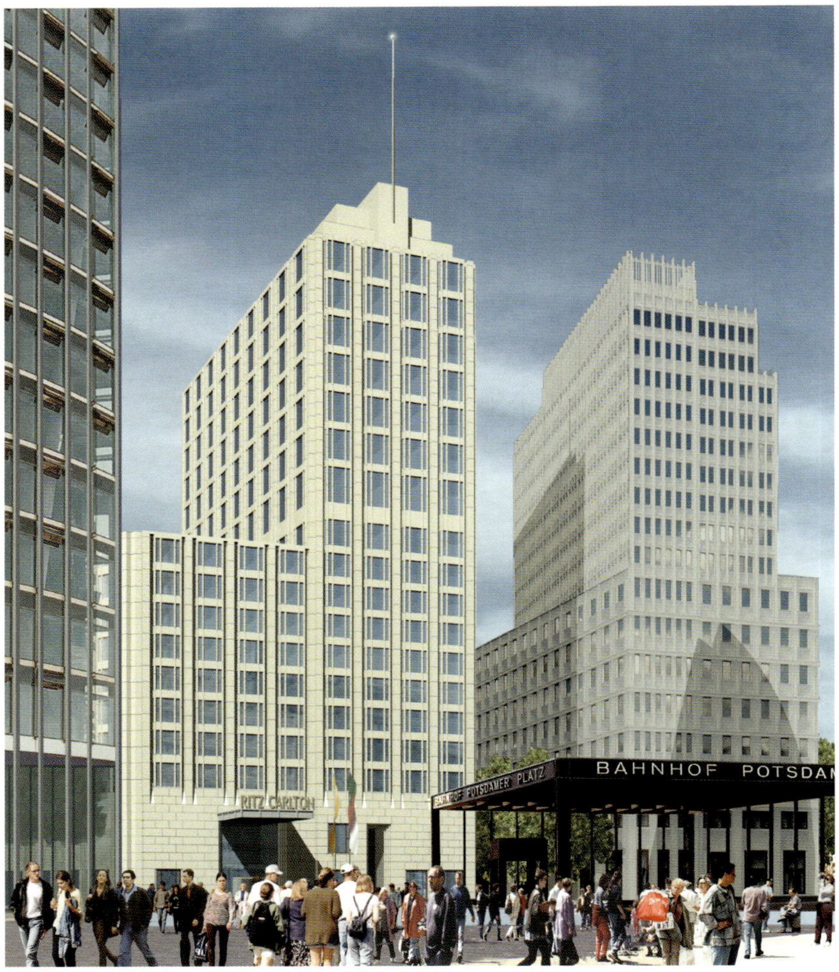

Hotelhochhaus Beisheim Center
Hilmer + Sattler + Albrecht, Berlin
2001–2004
Potsdamer Platz
Hotel · hotel · hotel

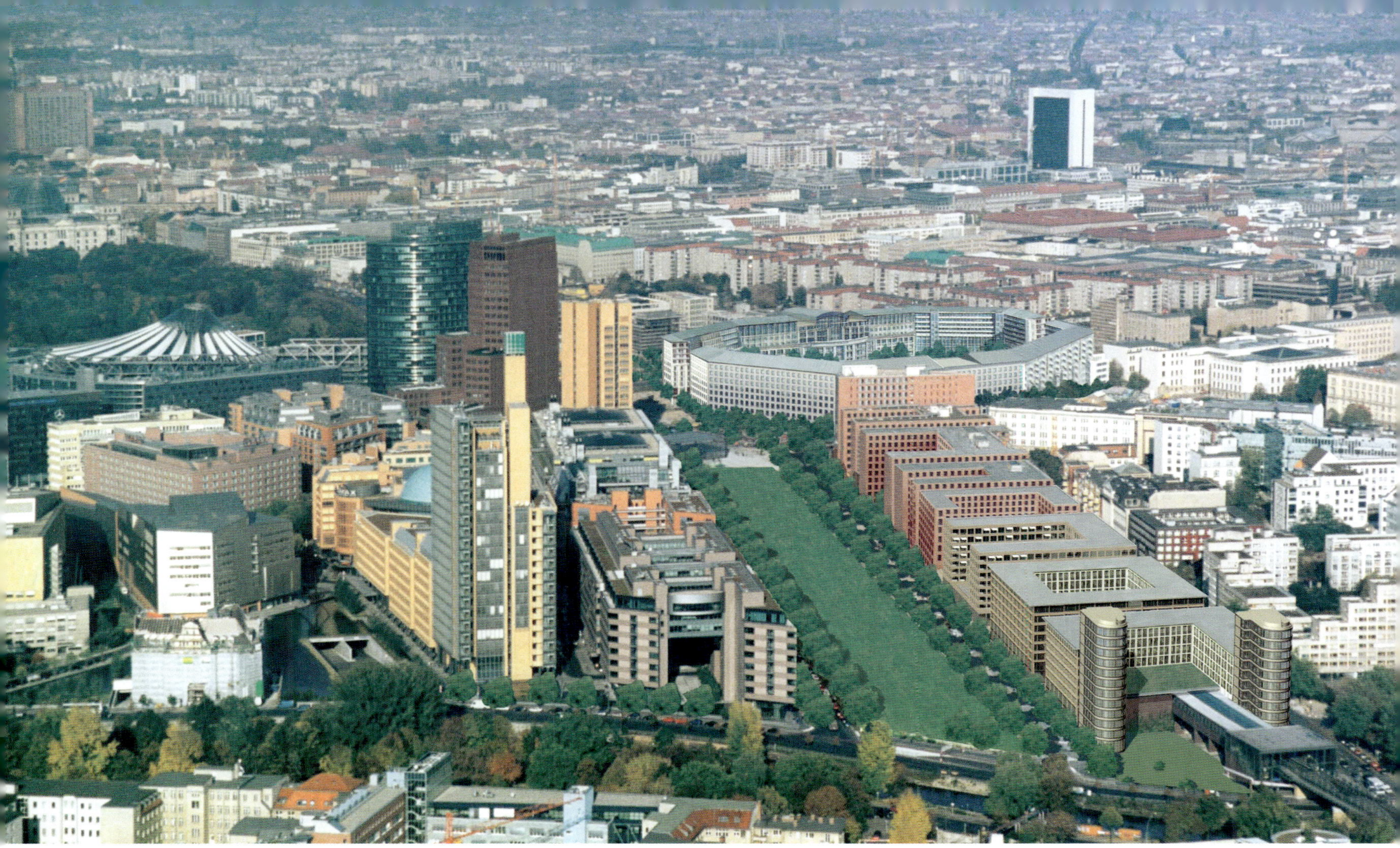

Simulation Potsdamer Platz von Südwesten mit Bebauung des Leipziger Platzes und der Gabriele-Tergit-Promenade
Simulation of Potsdamer Platz from the south-east with the development of Leipziger Platz and the Gabriele-Tergit-Promenade
Simulación del Potsdamer Platz desde el Suroeste con las construcciones del Leipziger Platz y del paseo Gabriele-Tergit

Park Kolonnaden
Giorgio Grassi, Mailand
1998–2000
Köthener Straße
Büro, Gewerbe, Wohnen
Office, business, residence
Oficinas, comercio, viviendas

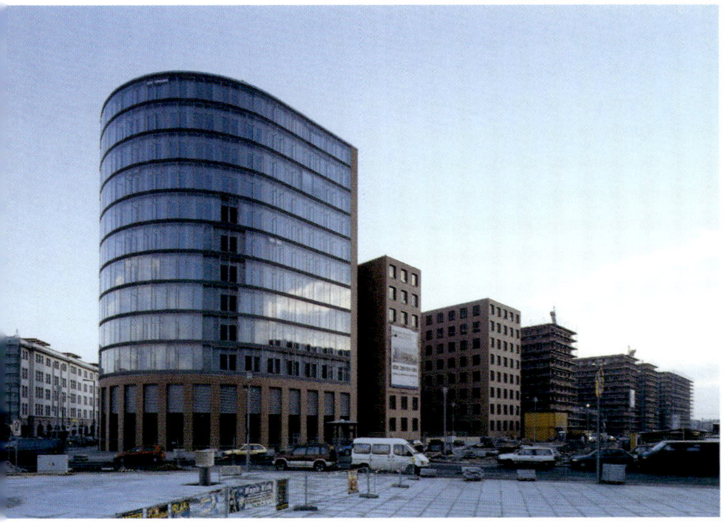

Projekt Gabriele-Tergit-Promenade
Hilmer + Sattler + Albrecht, Berlin
Gabriele-Tergit-Promenade
2001–2004
Büro, Gewerbe
Office, business
Oficinas, comercio

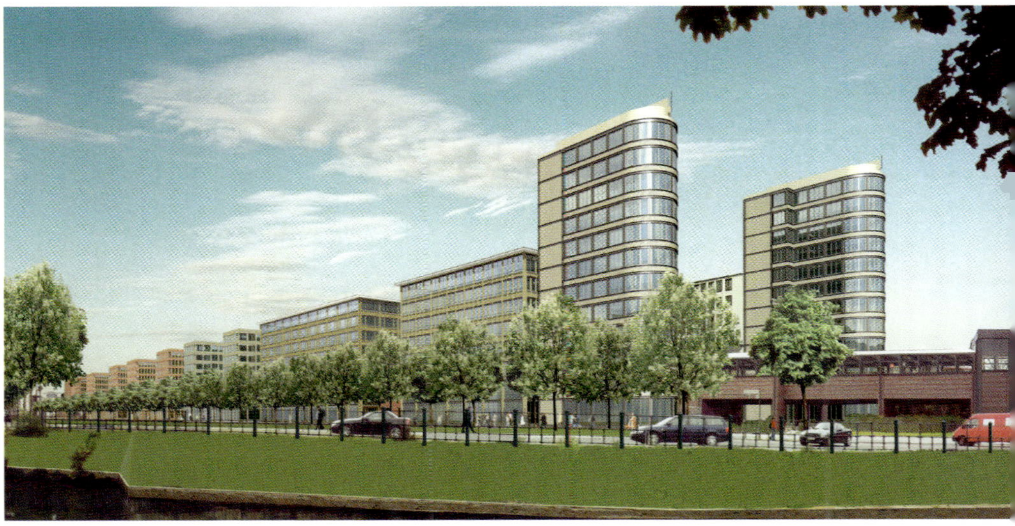

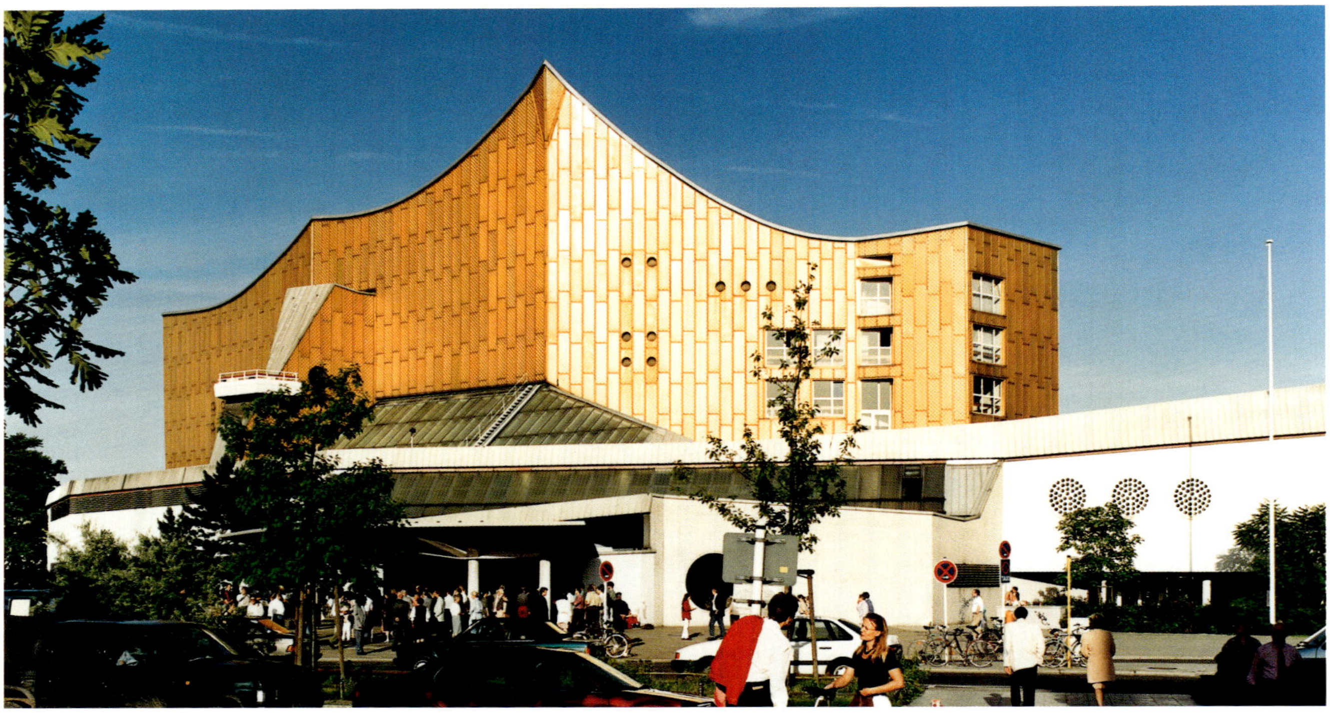

Philharmonie
Hans Scharoun
1960–1963
Herbert-von-Karajan-Straße
Konzertsaal · concert hall · sala de concierto

Blick über die Piazetta des Kulturforums auf den Potsdamer Platz
View over the Piazetta of the Kulturforum onto Potsdamer Platz
Vista del Potsdamer Platz con la plaza del Kulturforum en primer plano

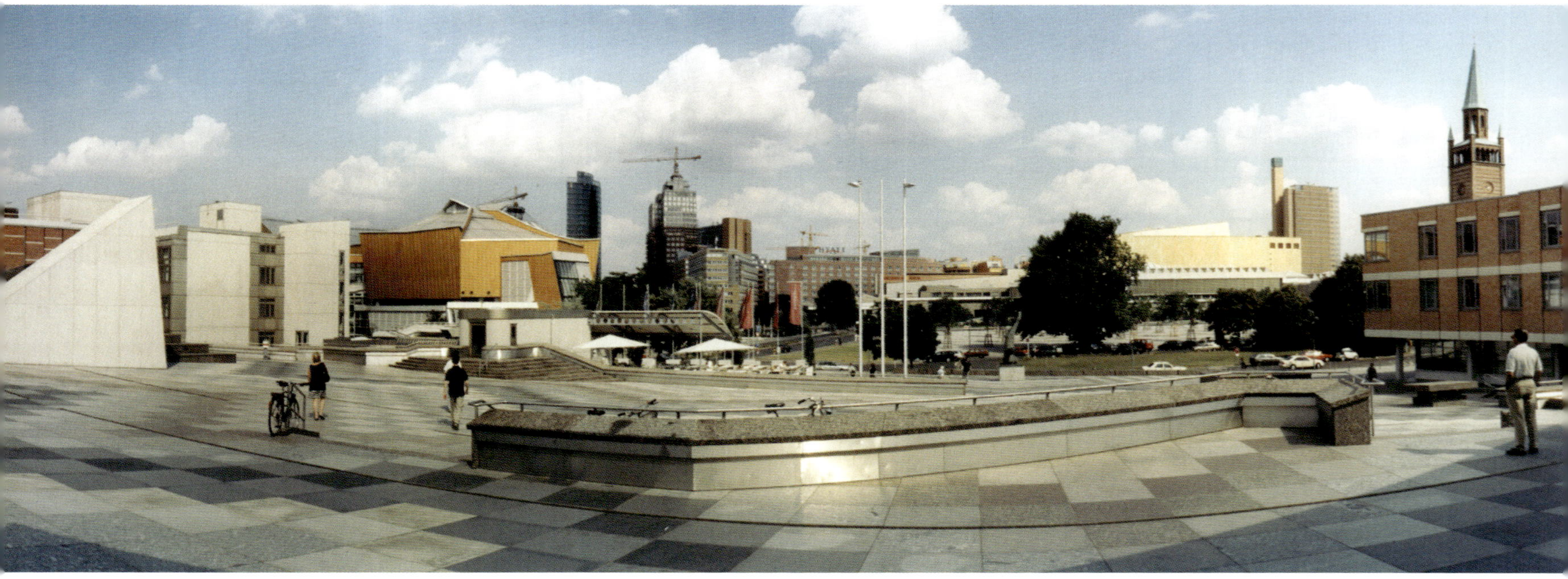

Neue Nationalgalerie und St. Matthäi-Kirche
Ludwig Mies van der Rohe, August Stüler
1965–1968,
1844–1864
Potsdamer Straße · Matthäikirchplatz
Museum · museum · museo

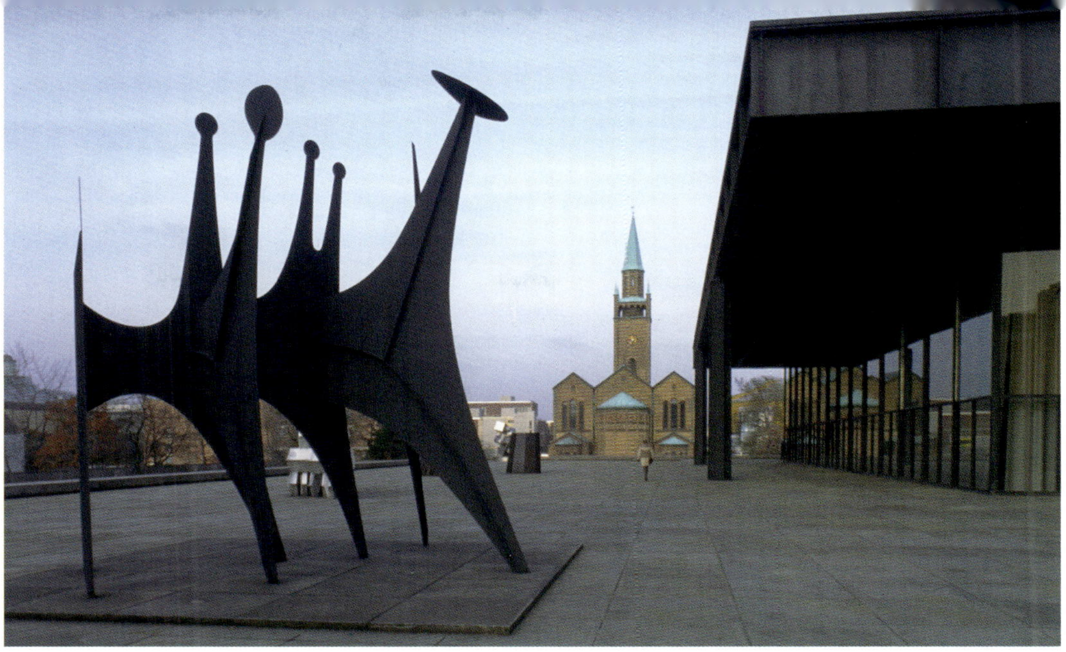

Zentrale Eingangshalle zum Kulturforum
Central entrance of the Kulturforum
Hall central de entrada en el Kulturforum
Hilmer & Sattler
(mit Thomas Albrecht), München/Berlin
1992–1998
Matthäikirchplatz

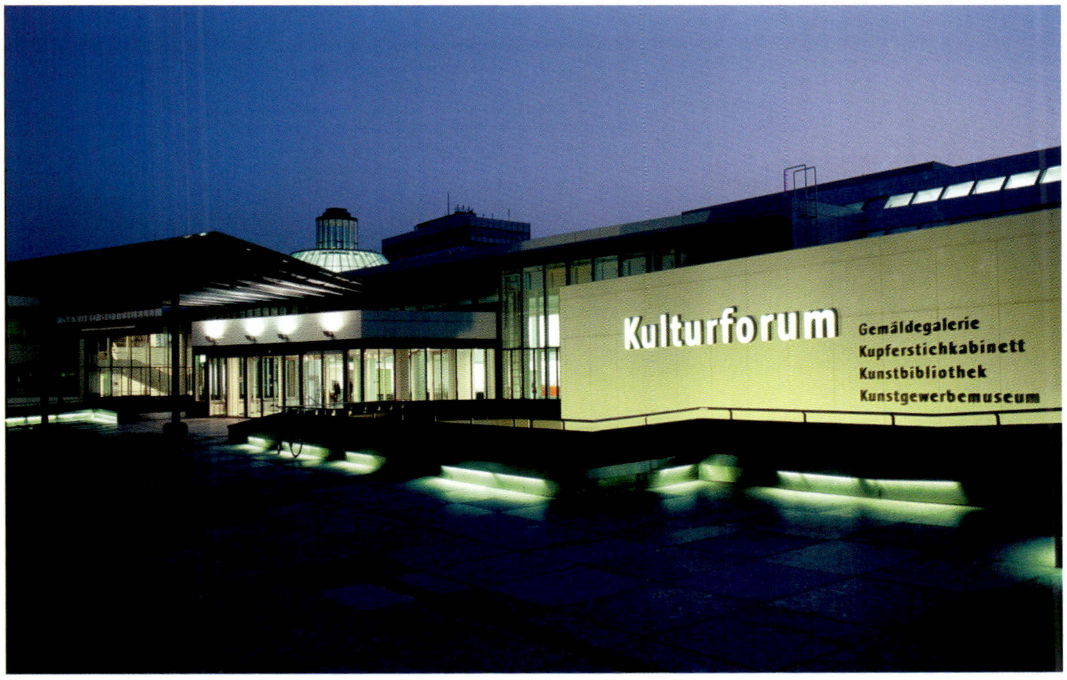

Gemäldegalerie
Hilmer & Sattler mit T. Albrecht, München/Berlin
1992–1998
Matthäikirchplatz · Sigismundstraße
Museum · museum · museo

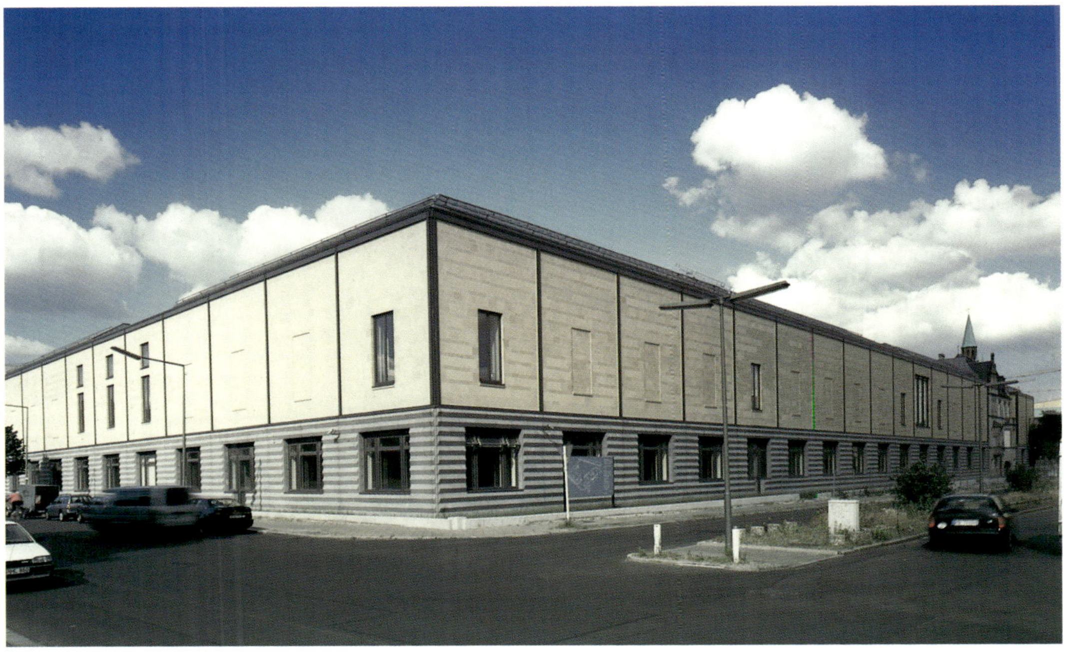

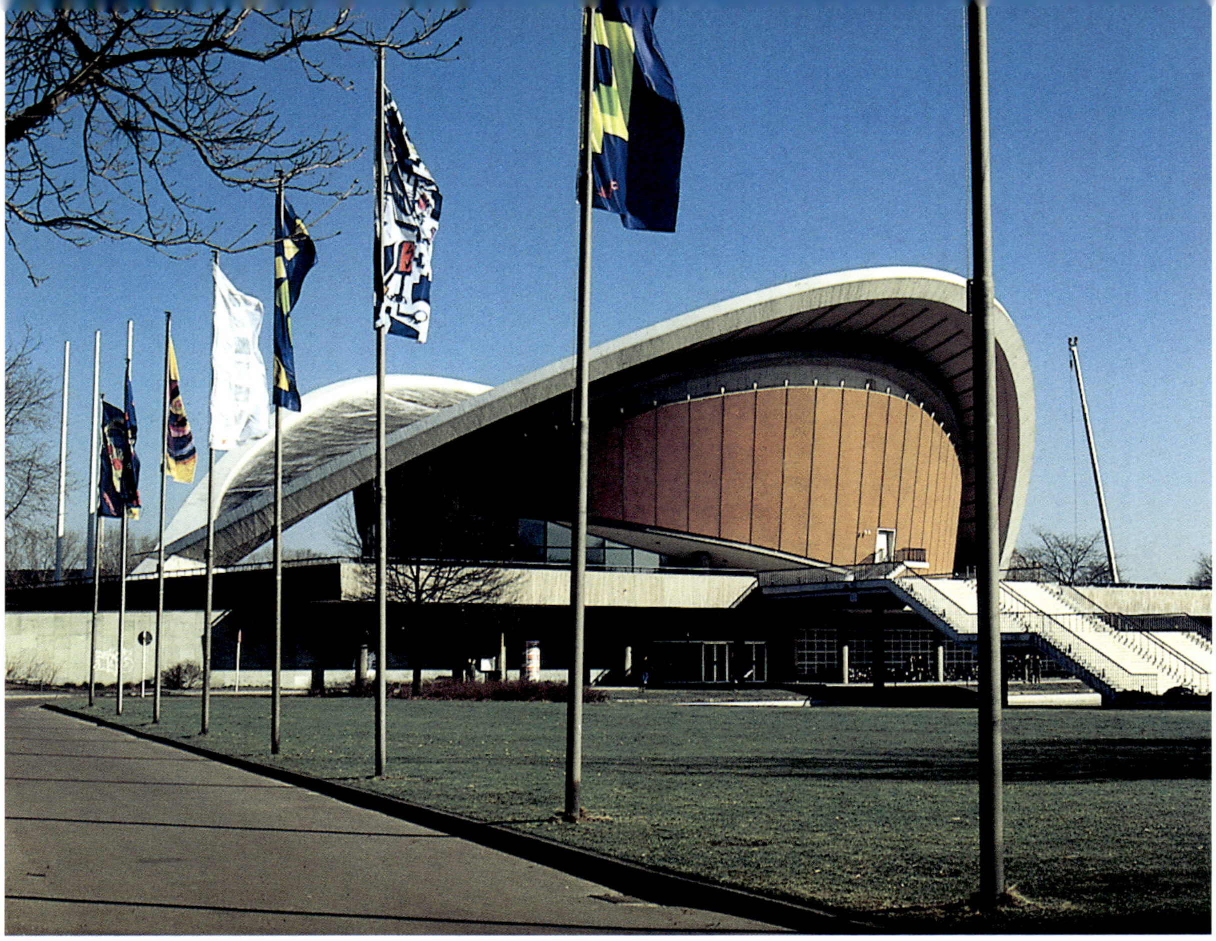

Haus der Kulturen der Welt
(Ehemalige · former · antiguo
Kongresshalle)
Hugh Stubbins
1956–1957
John-Foster-Dulles-Allee
Kultur · culture · cultura

Bundespräsidialamt
The Federal President's Office
Sede de la Presidencia Federal
Architekten Gruber, Kleine-Kraneburg, Frankfurt/Main
1996–1998
Spreeweg

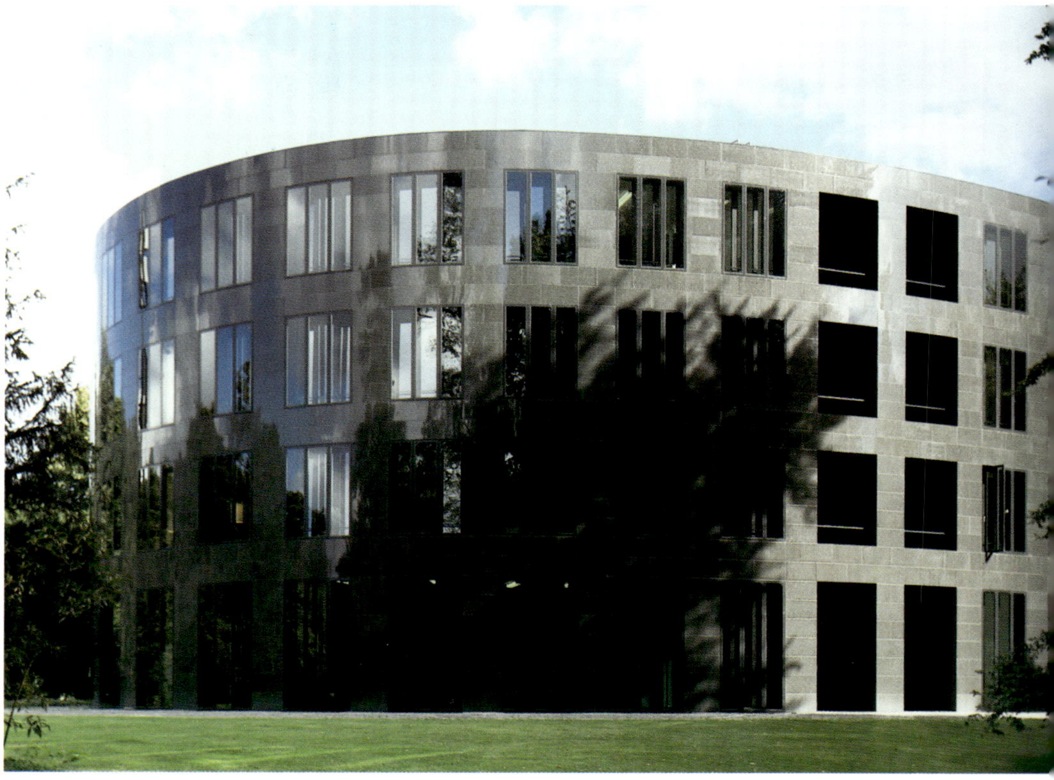

Großer Stern mit Siegessäule
Johann Heinrich Strack,
Friedrich Drake
1864, 1873
Kriegsdenkmal
War memorial
Monumento de Guerra

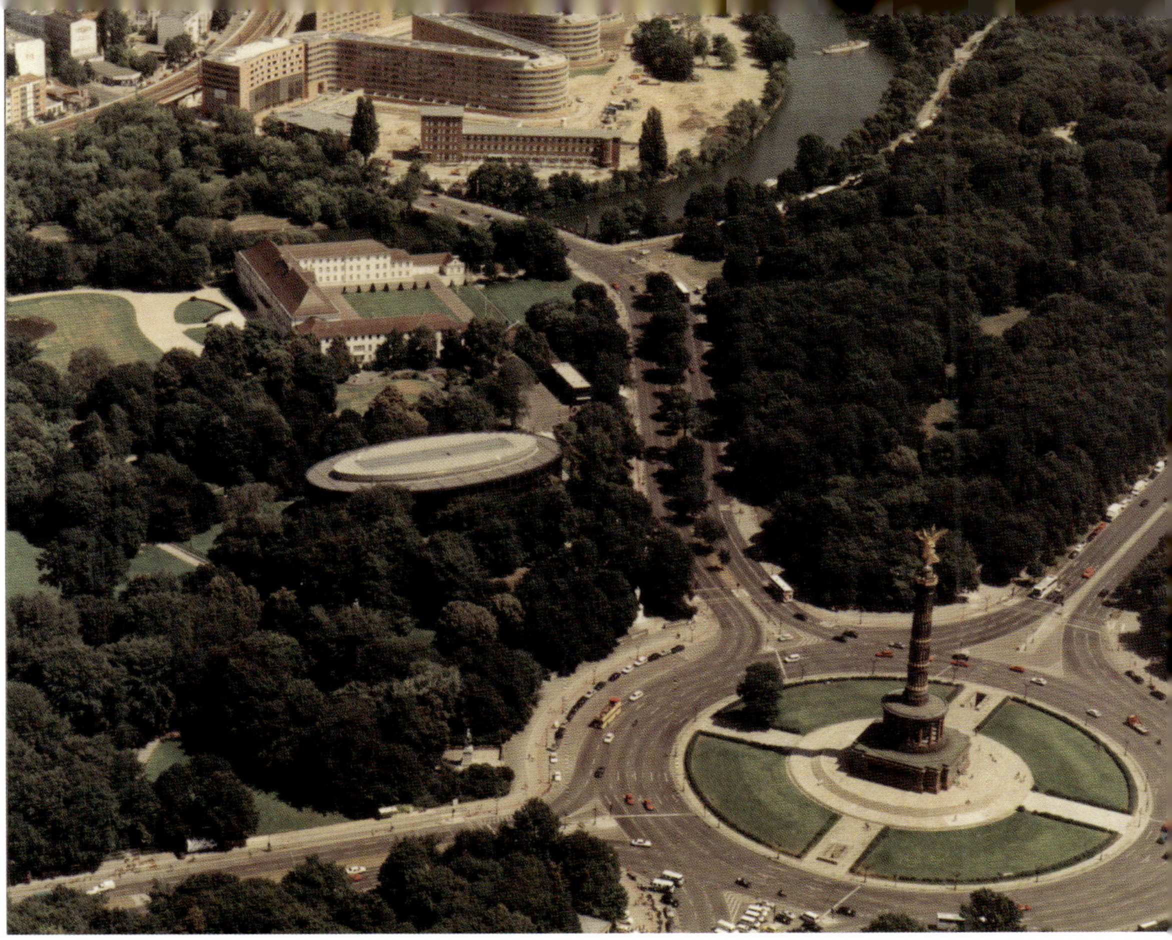

Schloss Bellevue
Michael Philipp Daniel Boumann
1785–1786
Spreeweg
Amtsitz des Bundespräsidenten
Official residence of the
Federal President
Residencia del Presidente Federal

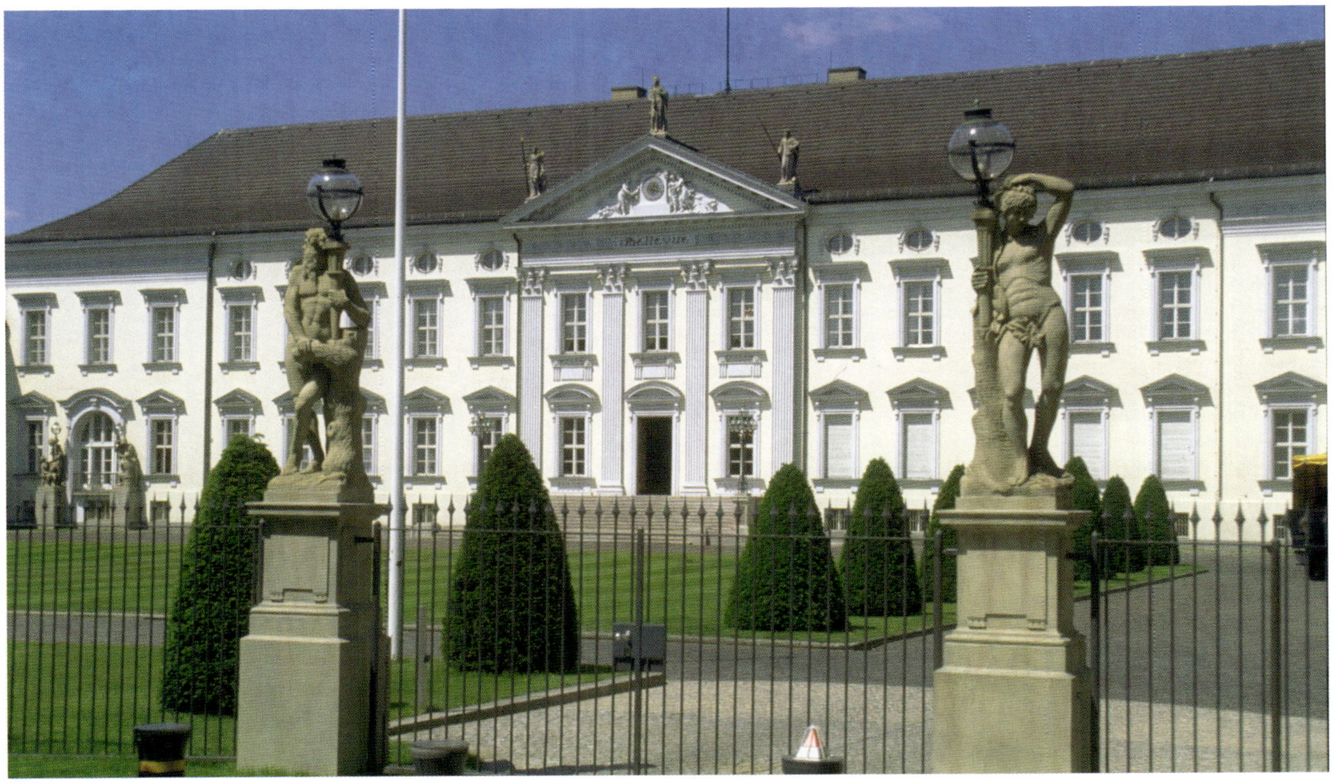

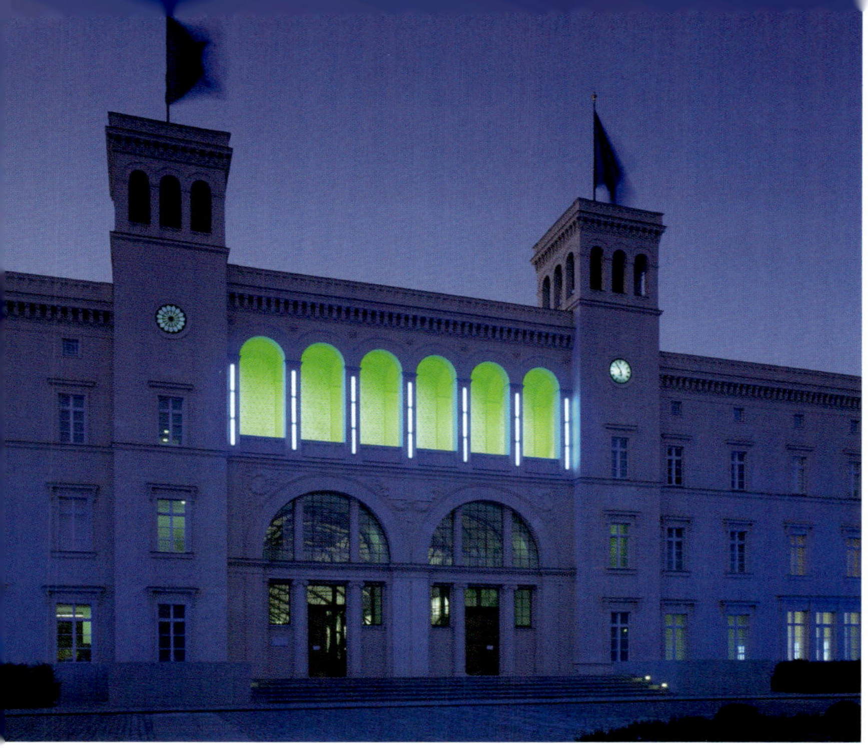

Hamburger Bahnhof
FRIEDRICH NEUHAUS,
FERDINAND WILHELM HOLZ,
JOSEF PAUL KLEIHUES
1845–1847,
1992–1997
Invalidenstraße
Museum für Gegenwart
Museum for the Present Berlin
Museo Contemporáneo

Ehemalige Kaiser-Wilhelm-Akademie
Antigua Academia del Kaiser Guillermo
WILHELM CREMER, RICHARD WOLFFENSTEIN
(Altbau · old building · edificio original),
THOMAS BAUMANN und DIETER SCHNITTGER, Berlin
(Um- und Neubau · alteration and extension · reforma y construcción nueva)
1903–1910, 1996–2000
Invalidenstraße · Scharnhorststraße
Bundesministerium für Wirtschaft und Technologie
Federal Ministry of Economic Affairs and Technology
Ministerio Federal de Economía y Tecnología

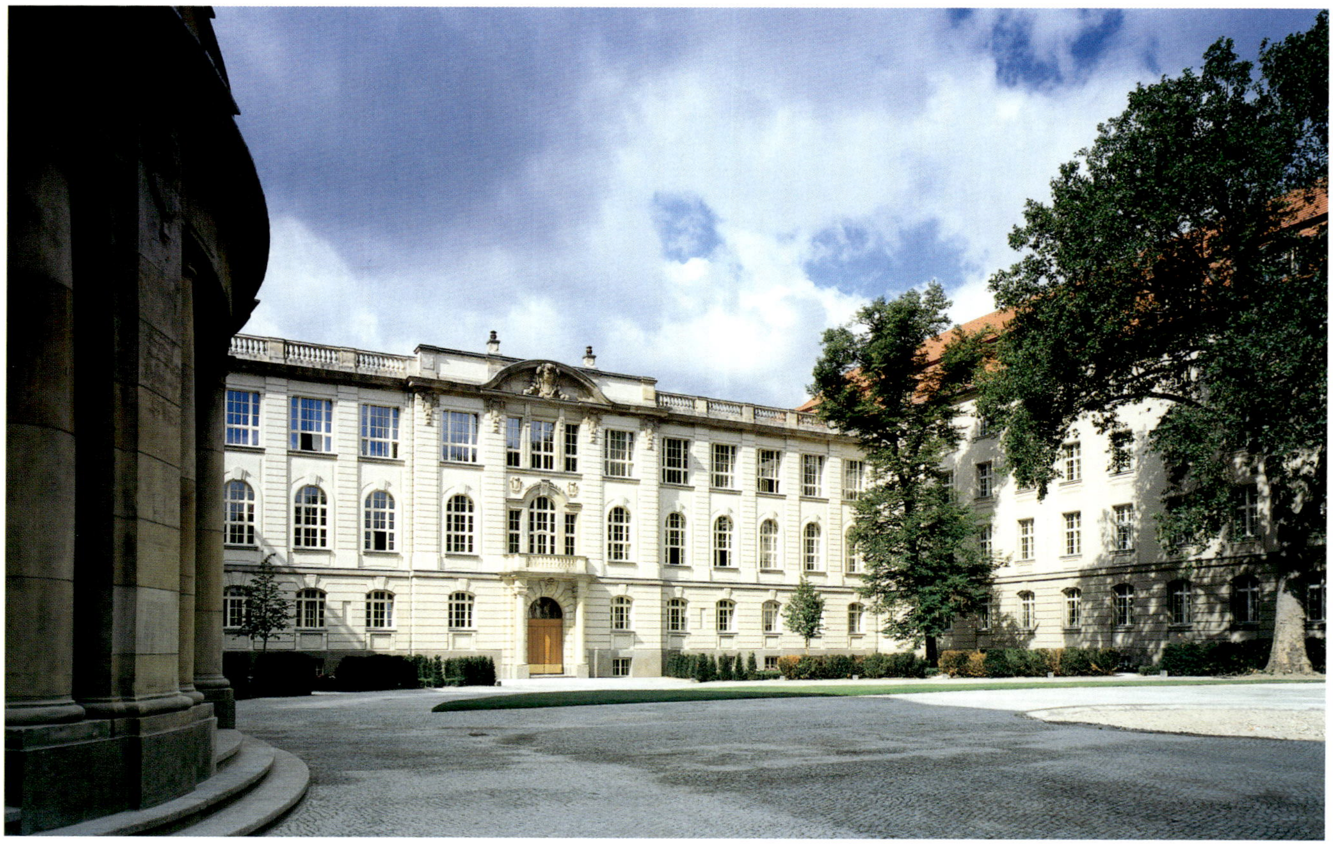

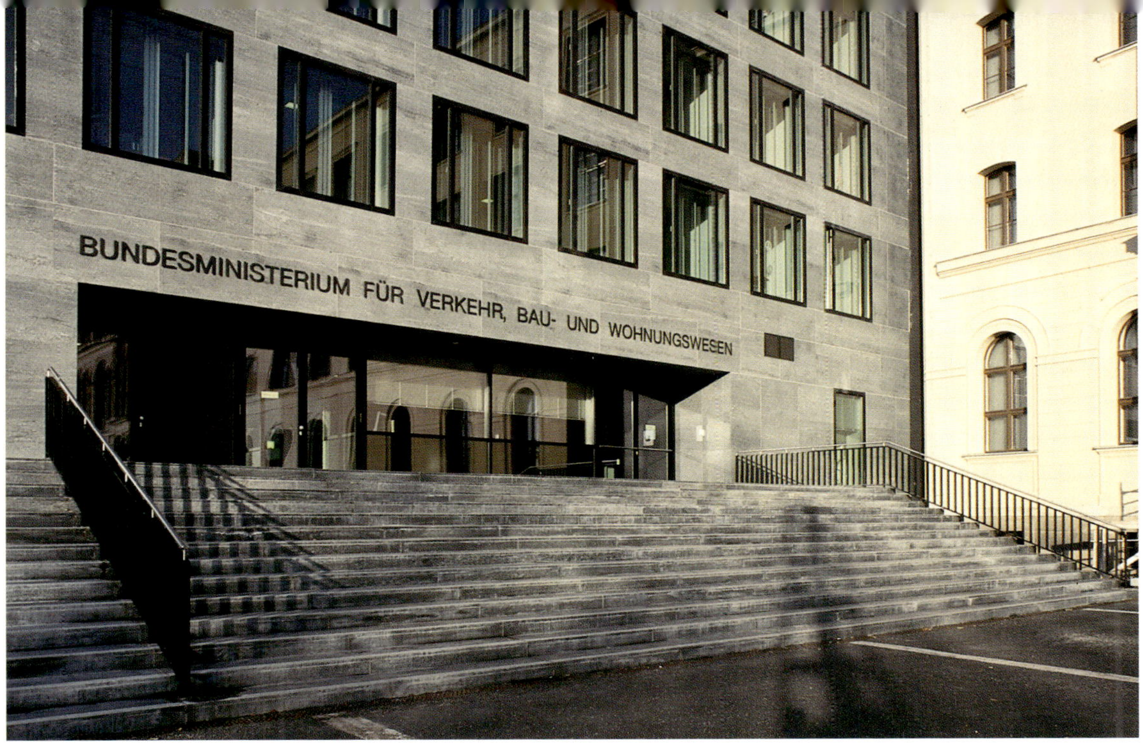

Ehemalige Geologische Landesanstalt
Former Geological State Institute
Antiguo Instituto de Geología
August Tiede (Altbau · old building · edificio original),
Gerber + Partner, Dortmund (Umbau · alteration · reforma),
Max Dudler, Zürich/Berlin (Neubau · new building · construcción nueva)
1874–1889,
1996–1999
Invalidenstraße
Bundesministerium für Verkehr, Bau- und Wohnungswesen
Federal Ministry of Transport, Construction and Residential Development
Ministerio Federal de Transportes, Construcción y Vivienda

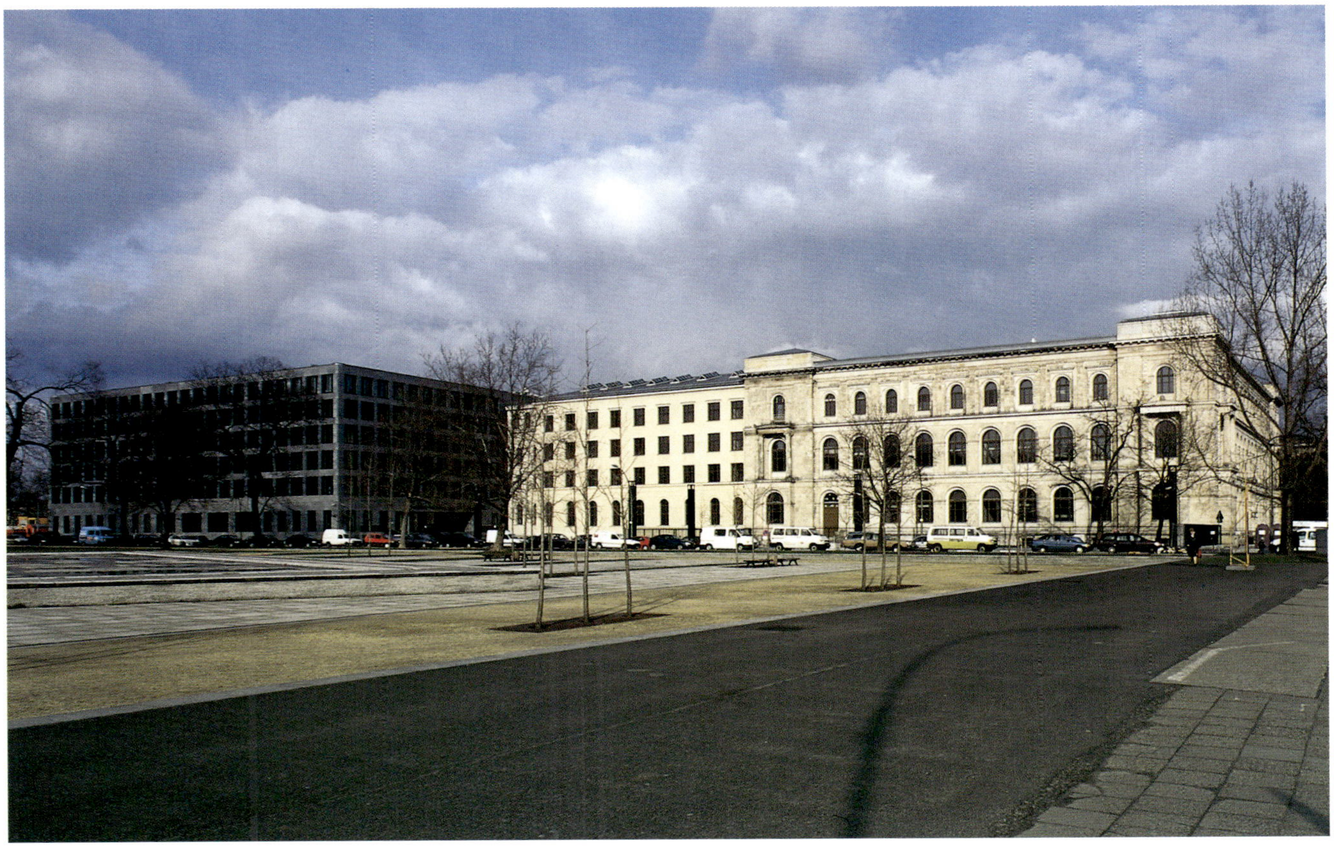

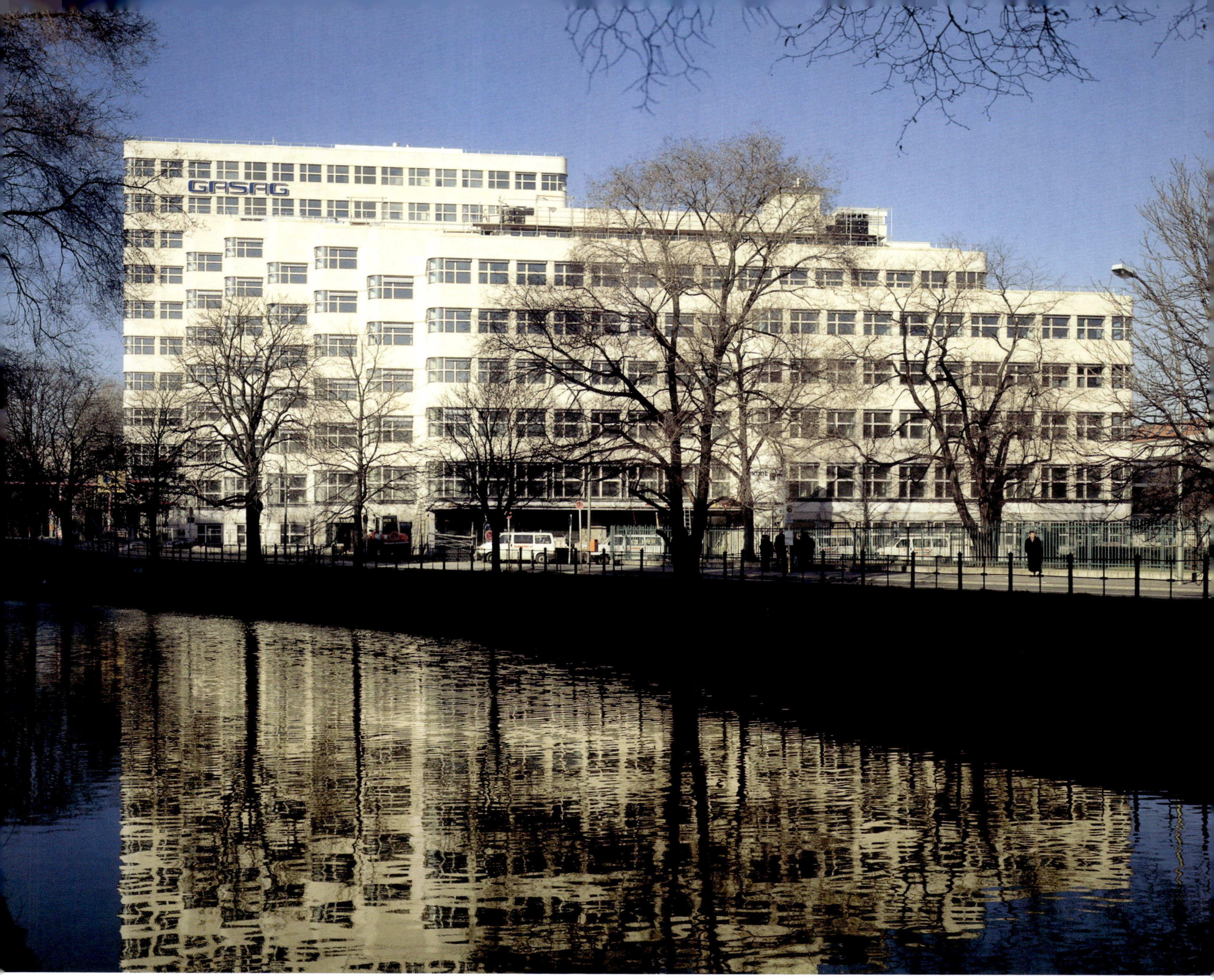

Shell-Haus
Emil Fahrenkamp
1930–1932
Reichpietschufer · Stauffenbergstraße
Büro · office · oficina

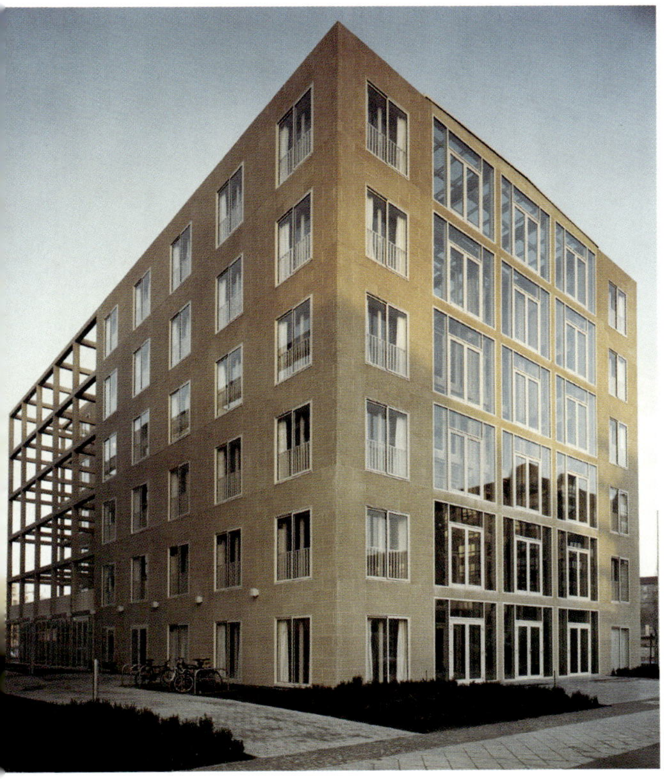

Landesvertretung des Saarlands
Federal State Offices of Saarland
Representación del Estado Federal del Sarre
Peter Alt und Thomas Britz, Saarbrücken
1999–2000
In den Ministergärten

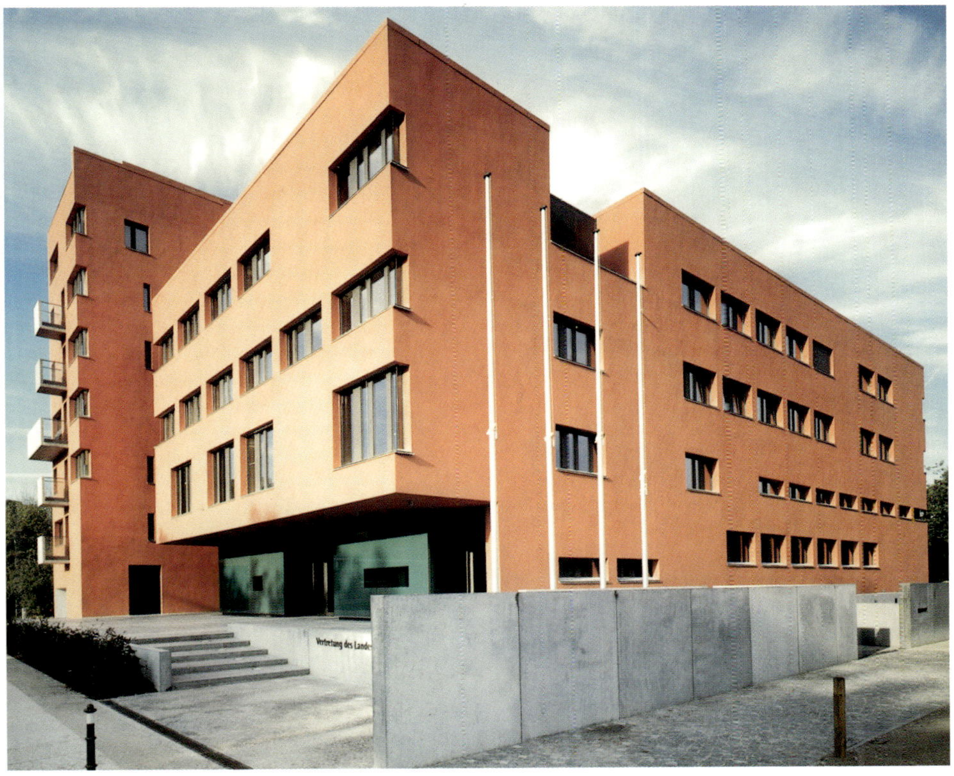

Landesvertretung der Freien und Hansestadt Bremen
Federal State Offices of the Hanseatic City of Bremen
Representación del Estado Federal del Estado Libre y Hanseático de Bremen
Léon Wohlhage Wernik Architekten, Berlin
1998–1999
Hiroshimastraße

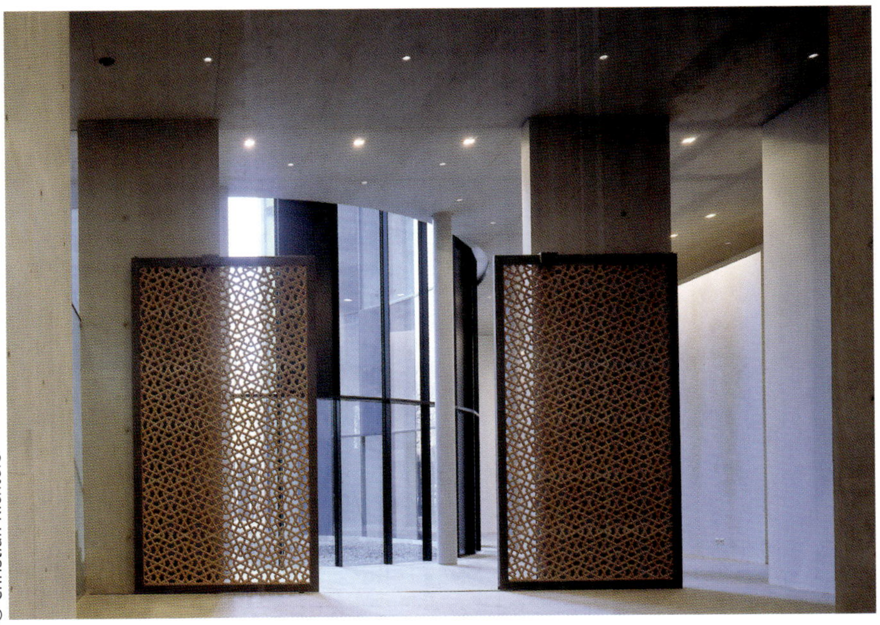

Botschaft von Indien (Innenansicht)
Embassy of India (interior view)
Embajada de India (vista interior)
Léon Wohlhage Wernik Architekten, Berlin
1999–2001
Tiergartenstraße

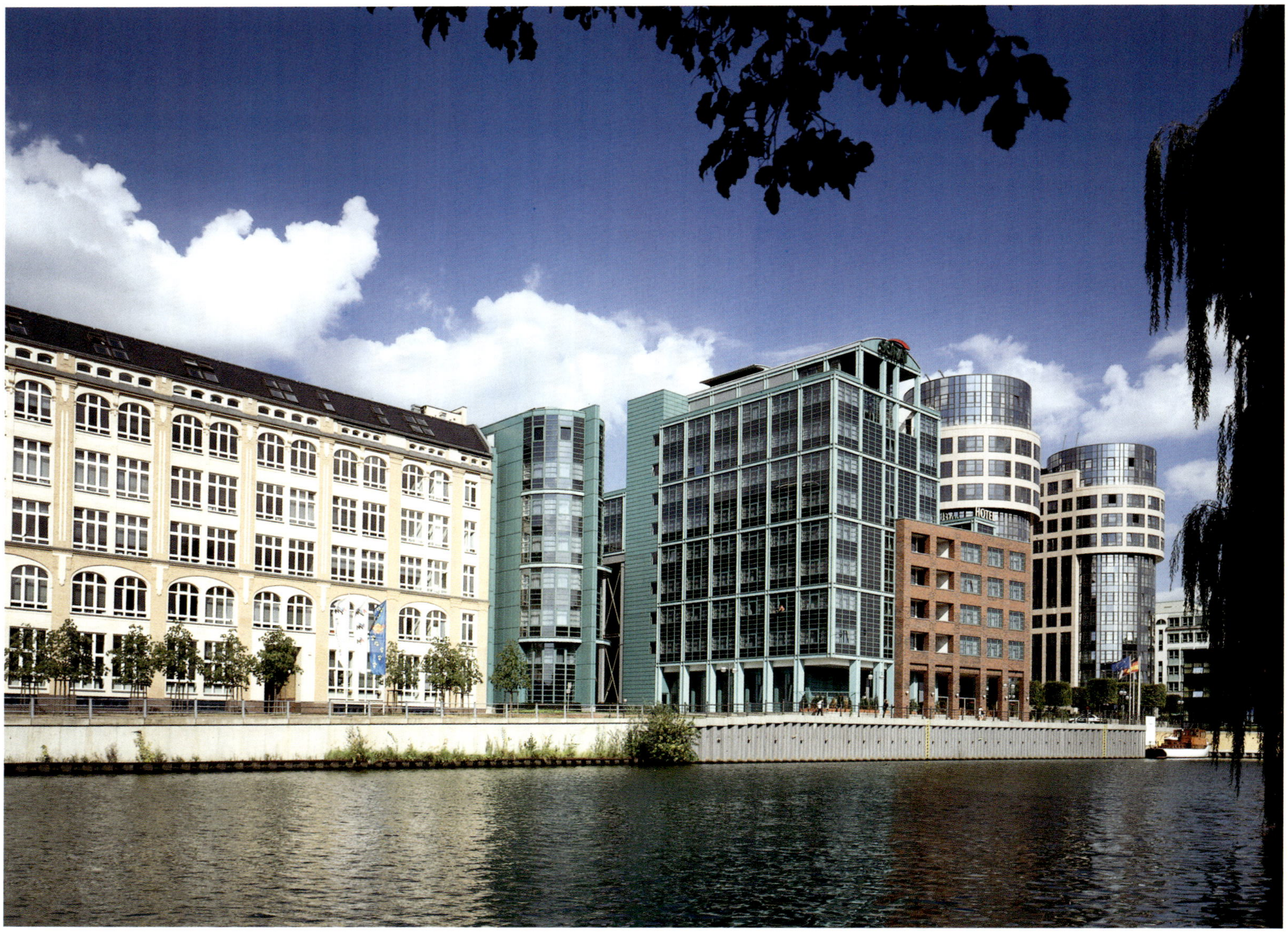

Von links nach rechts · from left to right · de izquierda a derecha:
Ufer-Haus (Altbau · old building · edificio original),
Alte Meierei (Erweiterung · extension · reforma) und Spree-Bogen
Wolf-Rüdiger Borchardt, Berlin (Alte Meierei),
Kühn-Bergander-Bley, Berlin (Spree-Bogen)
1992–1994 (Alte Meierei, Spree-Bogen)
Alt-Moabit
Sitz des Bundesministeriums des Innern
Seat of the Federal Ministry of the Interior
Sede del Ministerio Federal del Interior (Spree-Bogen)
Hotel · hotel · hotel (Alte Meierei)
Büro, Wohnen · office, residence · oficina, viviendas (Alte Meierei, Spree-Bogen)
Gewerbe · business · comercio (Ufer-Haus, Alte Meierei, Spree-Bogen)

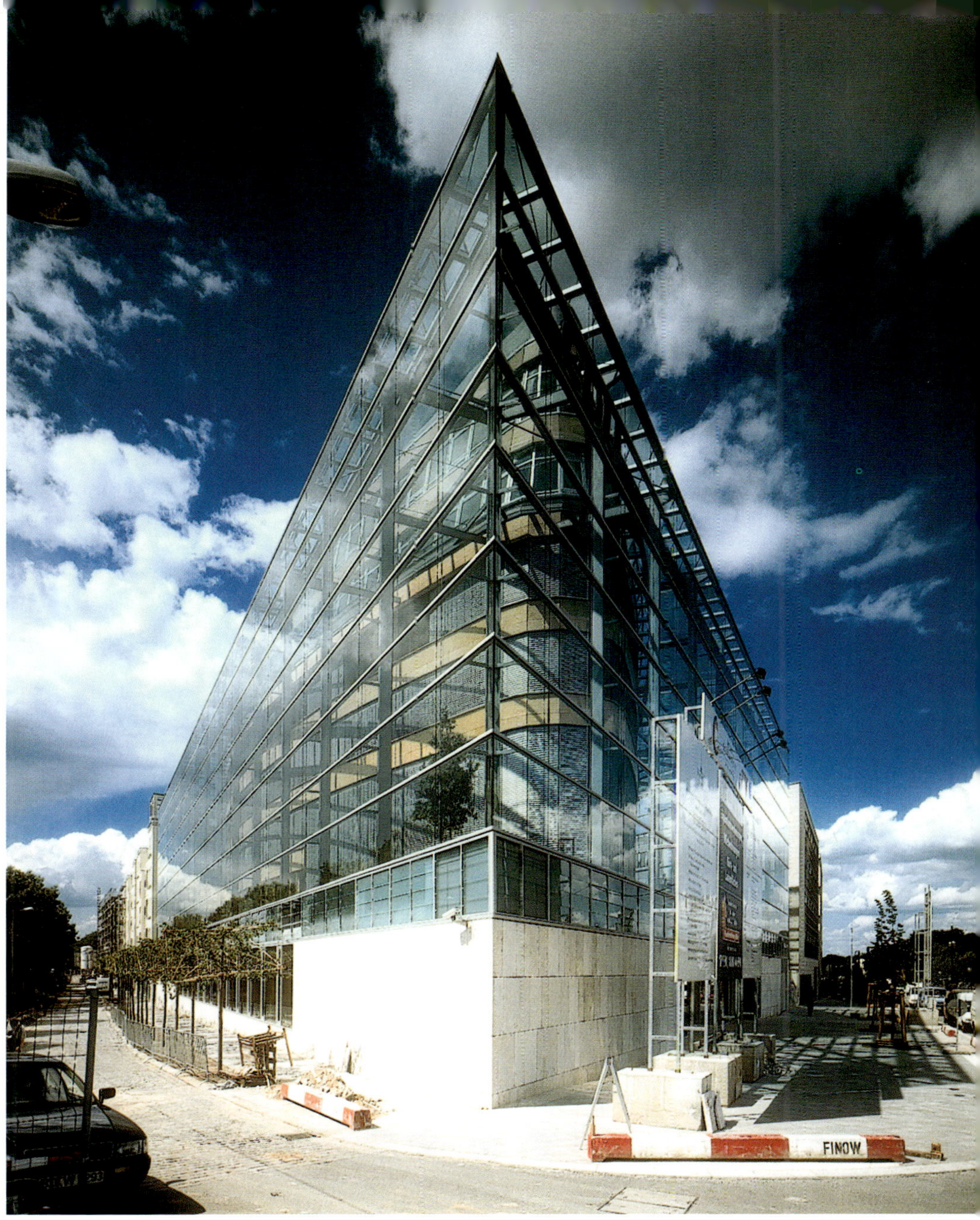

Bundesgeschäftsstelle der CDU
National Headquarters of the CDU
Sede de la Unión Demócrata Cristiana (CDU)
PETZINKA, PINK und Partner, Düsseldorf
1999–2000
Klingelhöferstraße · Corneliusstraße

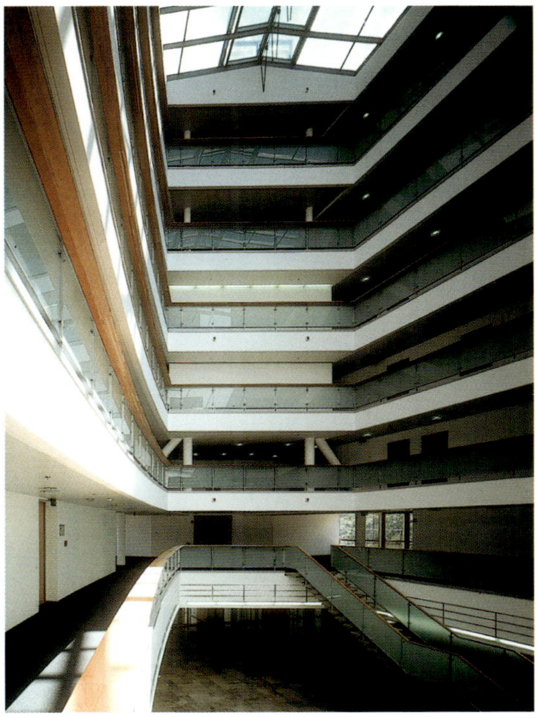

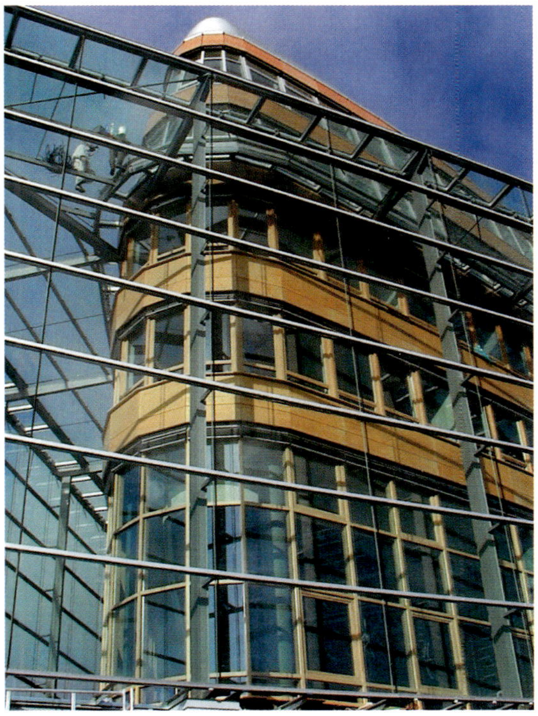

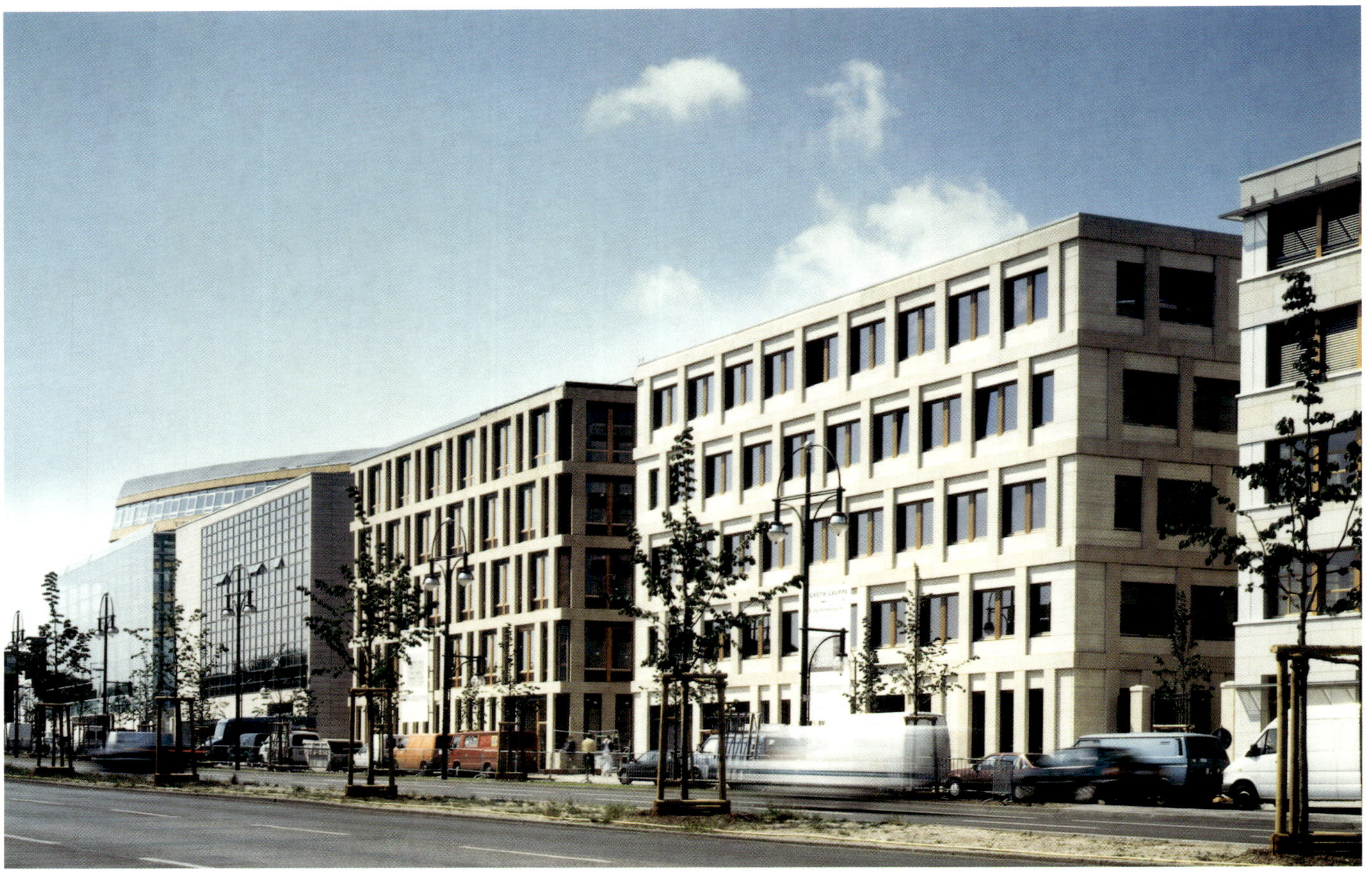

Tiergarten Dreieck
Von links nach rechts · from left to right · de izquierda a derecha: Bundesgeschäftsstelle der CDU · National Headquarters of the CDU · Sede de la Unión Demócrata Cristiana (CDU); Botschaften von Luxemburg und Malta · Embassies of Luxembourg and Malta · Embajadas de Luxemburgo y Malta, Deutsches Verkehrsforum; Botschaft von Malaysia · Embassy of Malaysia · Embajada de Malasia; Württembergische Lebensversicherung
Sayed Mohammad Oreyzi, Köln (Luxemburg, Malta, Deutsches Verkehrsforum),
PSP Pysall Stahrenberg und Partner, Berlin (Malaysia),
Gesine Weinmiller, Berlin (Würtembergische Lebensversicherung)
1998–2000
Klingelhöferstraße

Botschaft der Vereinigten Staaten von Mexiko
Embassy of Mexico
Embajada de los Estados Unidos Mexicanos
Teodoro González de Léon, Francisco Serrano, Mexico-City
1999–2000
Klingelhöferstraße · Rauchstraße

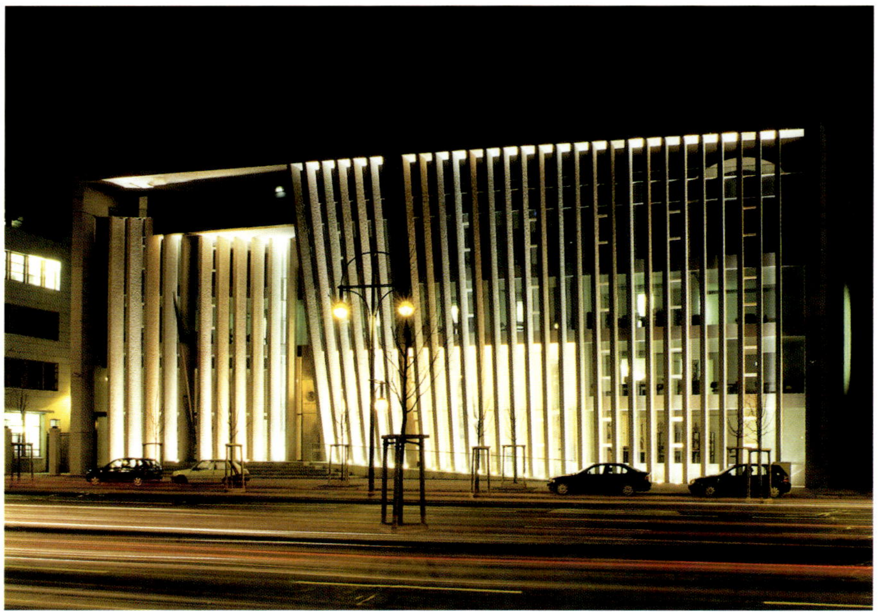

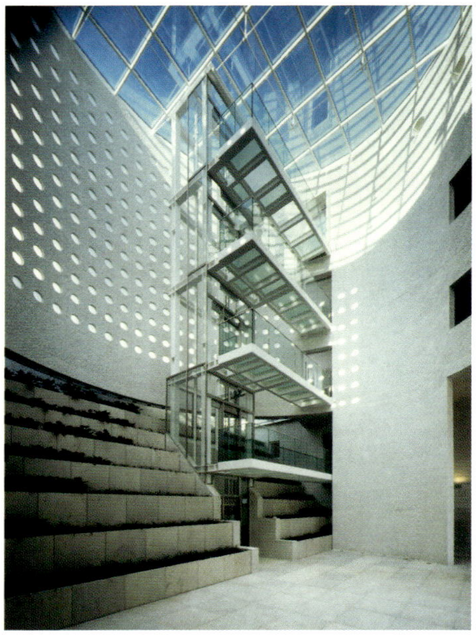

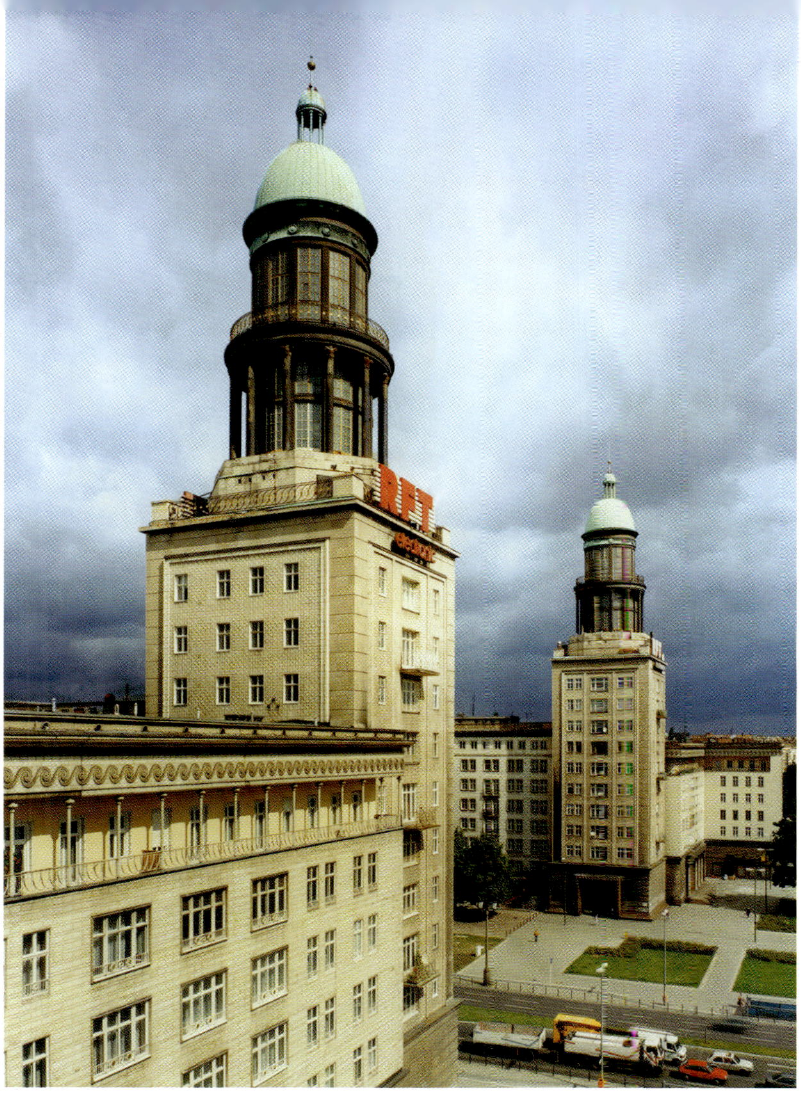

Ensemble der ehemaligen Stalinallee
HERRMANN HENSELMANN, RICHARD PAULICK, et.al.
1951–1960
Karl-Marx-Allee/Frankfurter Allee
Wohnen, Gewerbe
Residence, business
Viviendas, comercio

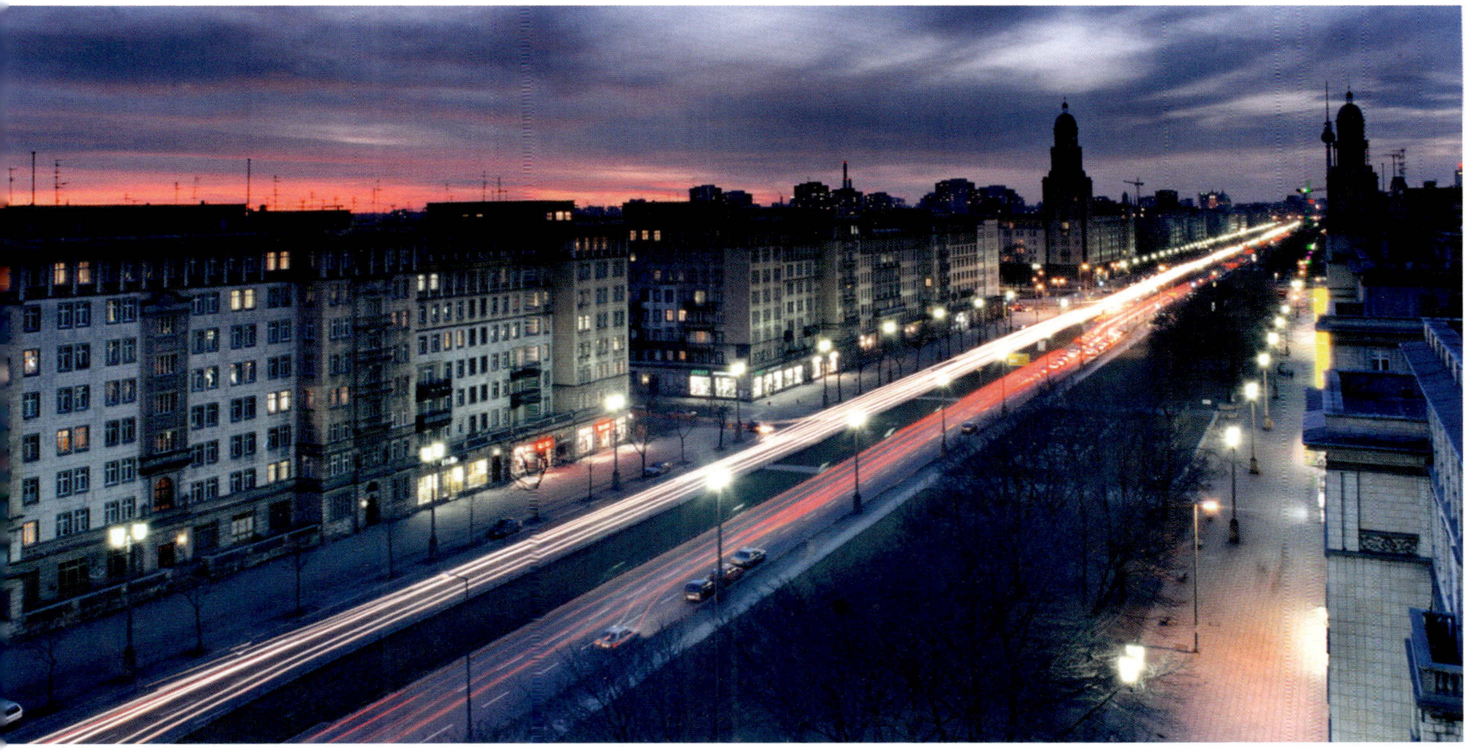

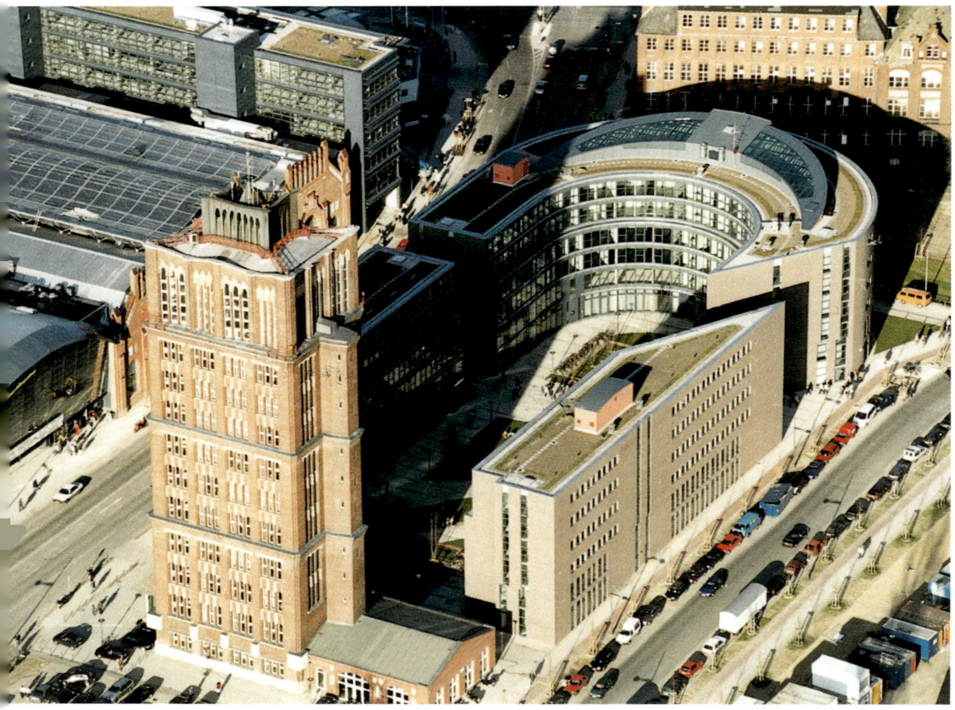

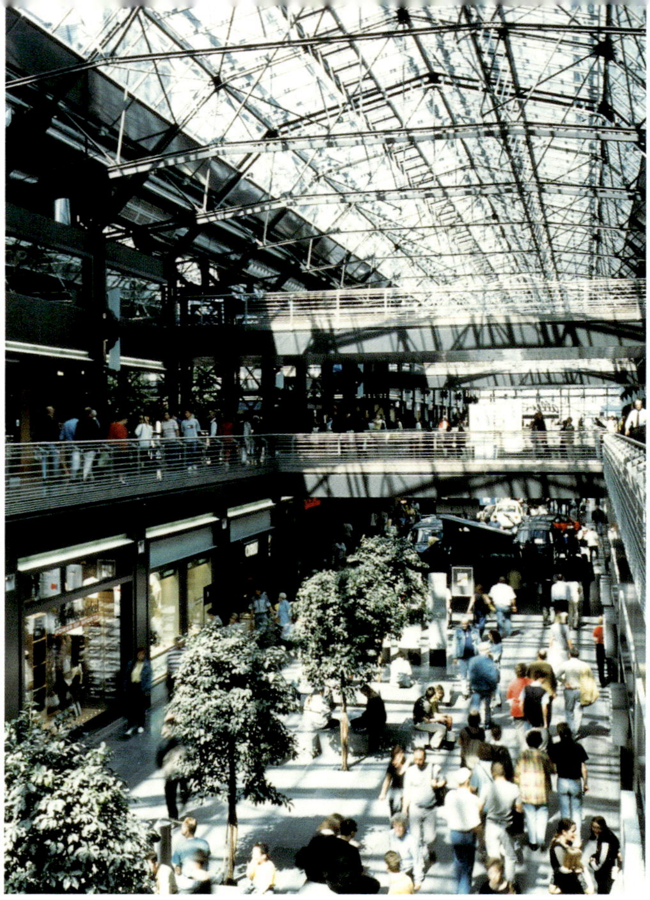

Wohn- und Gewerbegebiet »Am Borsigturm«
Norbert Stocker, Berlin, Rolfes & Partner, Berlin,
Axel Schultes/Deubzer und König, Berlin,
Claude Vasconi, Paris
1995–1999
Am Borsigturm
Büro, Gewerbe, Wohnen
Office, business, residence
Oficina, comercio, viviendas

Gewerbezentrum Ullsteinhaus
Nalbach + Nalbach, Berlin
1924, 1991–1995
Ullsteinstraße
Büro, Gewerbe
Office, business
Oficina, comercio

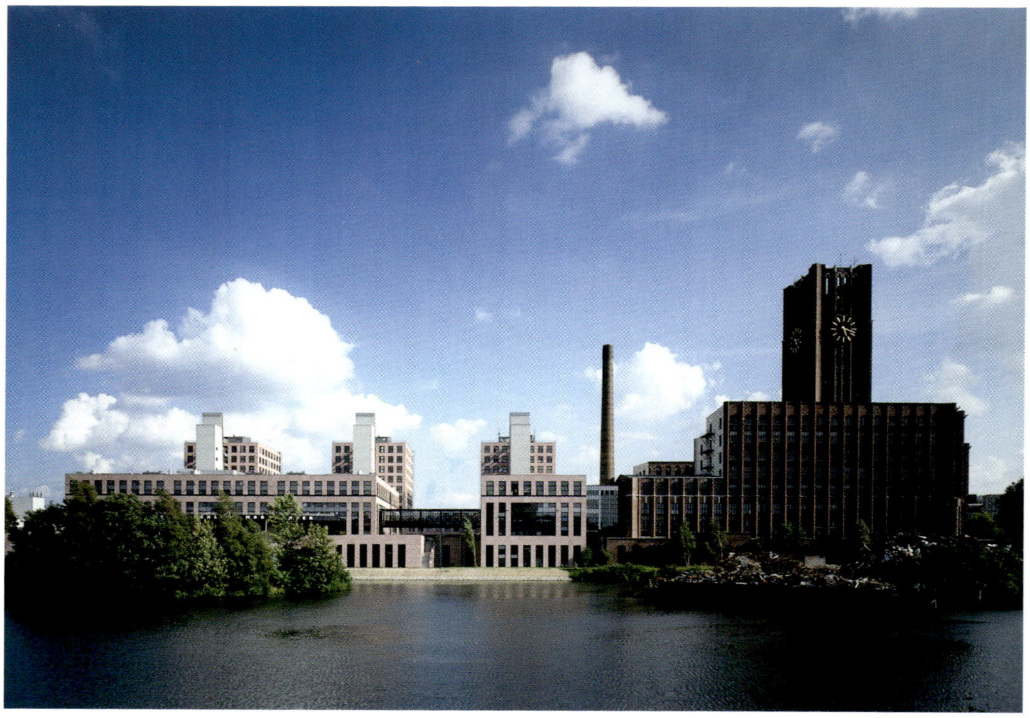

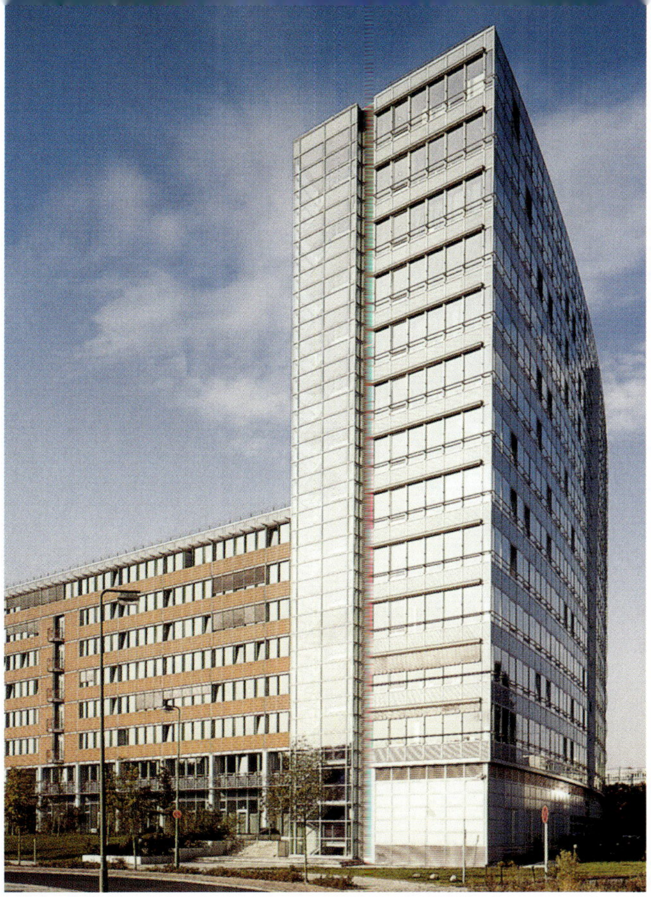

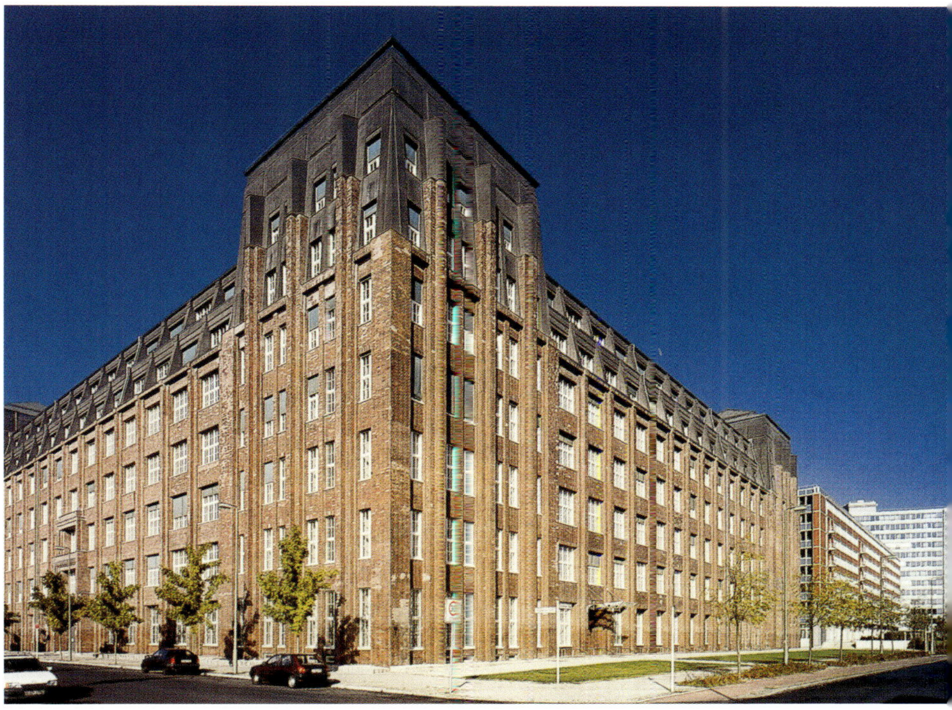

Dienstleistungszentrum Ostkreuz,
Sanierung und Erweiterung der ehemaligen KNORR-BREMSE AG
ALFRED GRENANDER, (Altbau · old building · edificio original),
J·S·K· Dipl. Ing. Architekten
(Erweiterung, Sanierung · extension and alteration · ampliación y reforma)
1922–1927,
1993–1995
Hirschberger Straße · Schreiberhauer Straße
Büro, Gewerbe
Office, business
Oficina, comercio

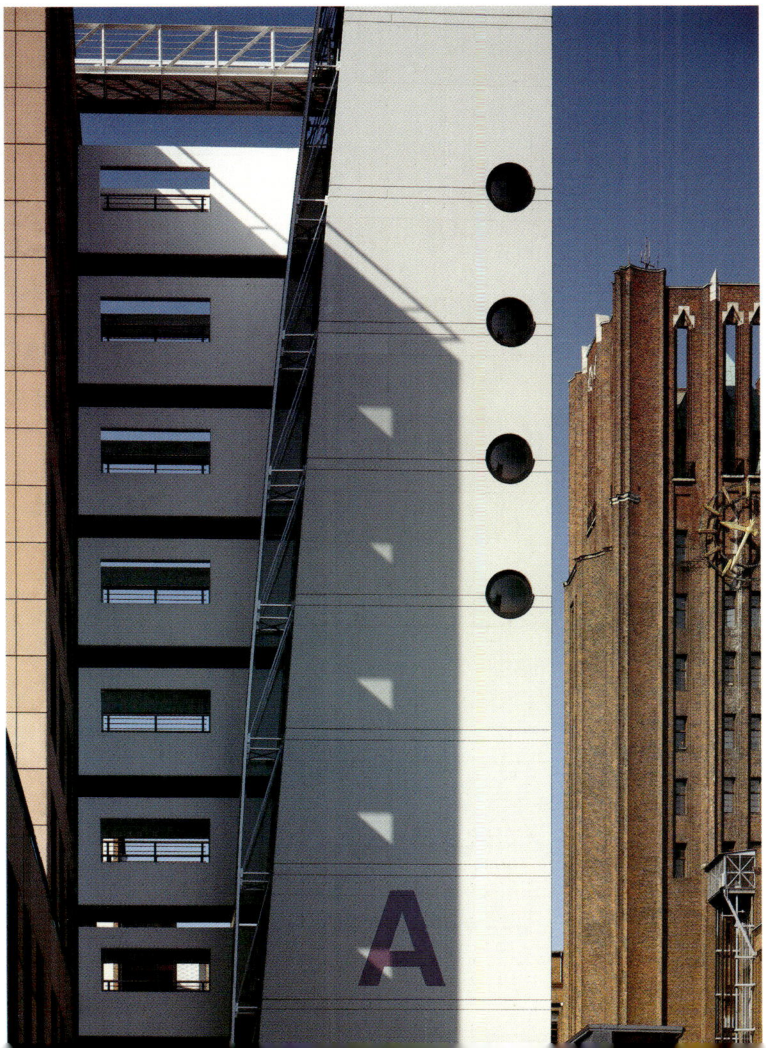

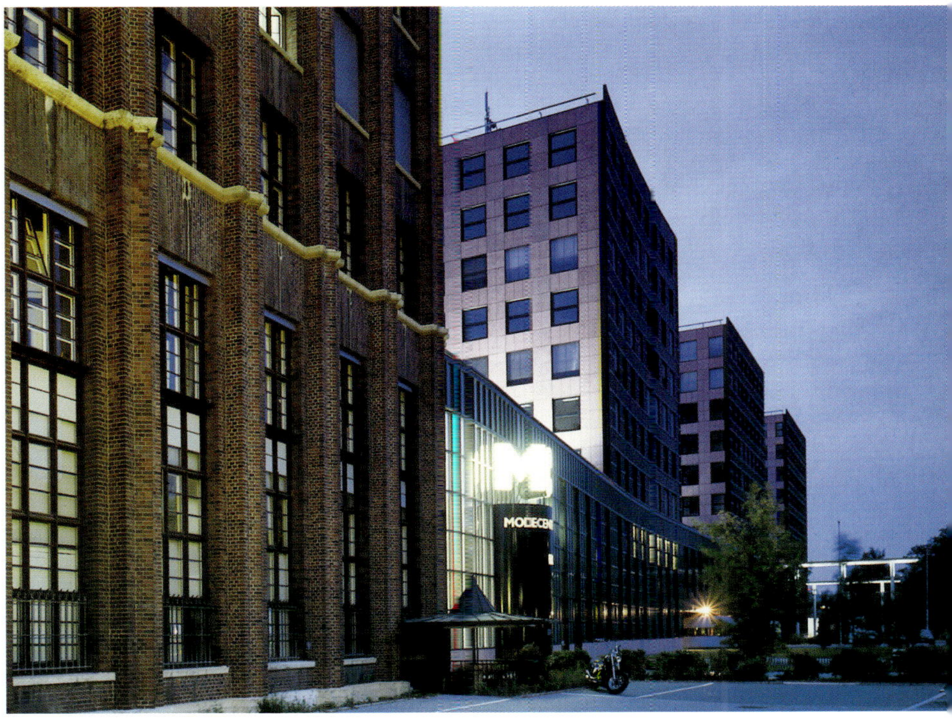

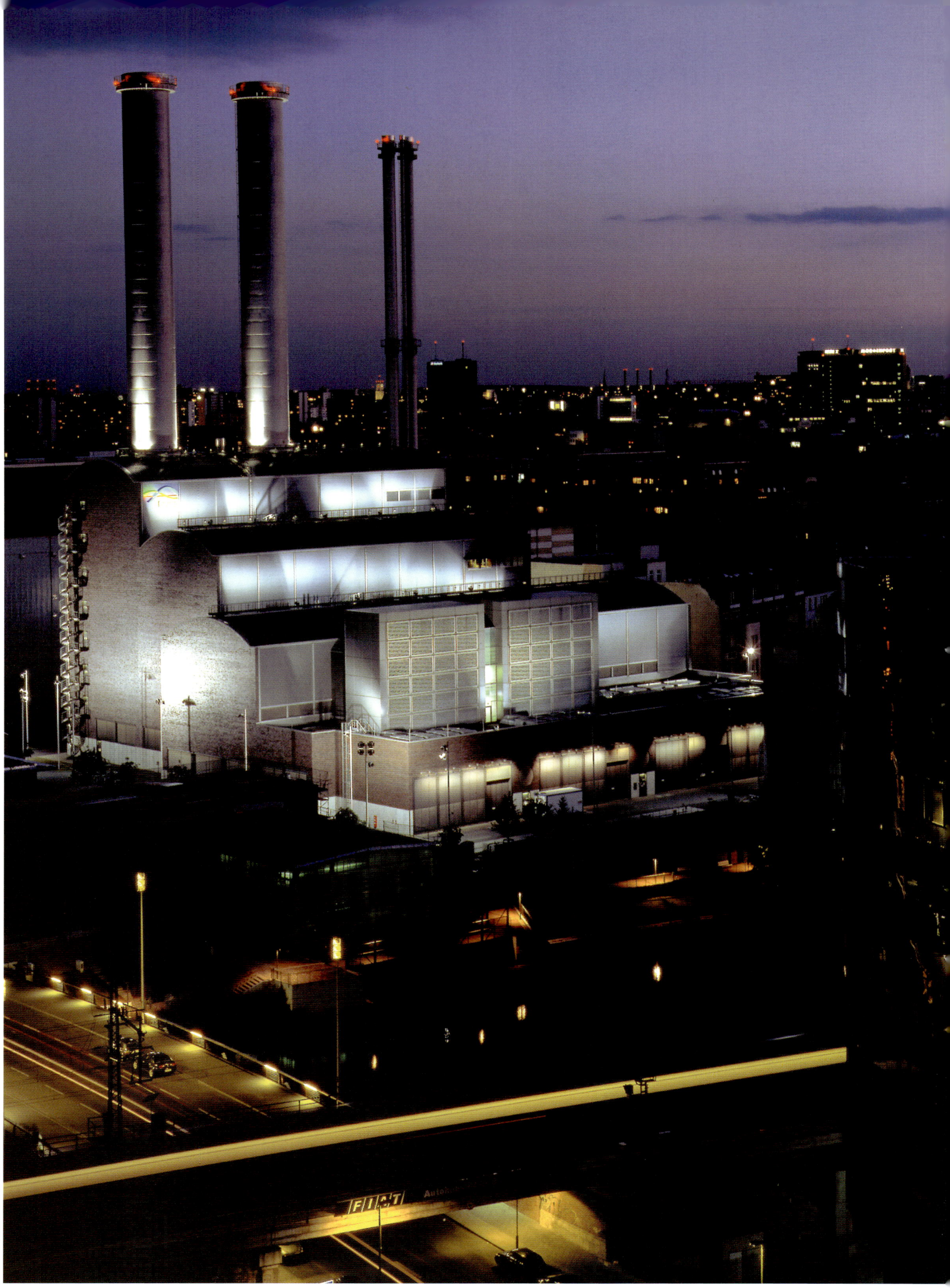
FIAT

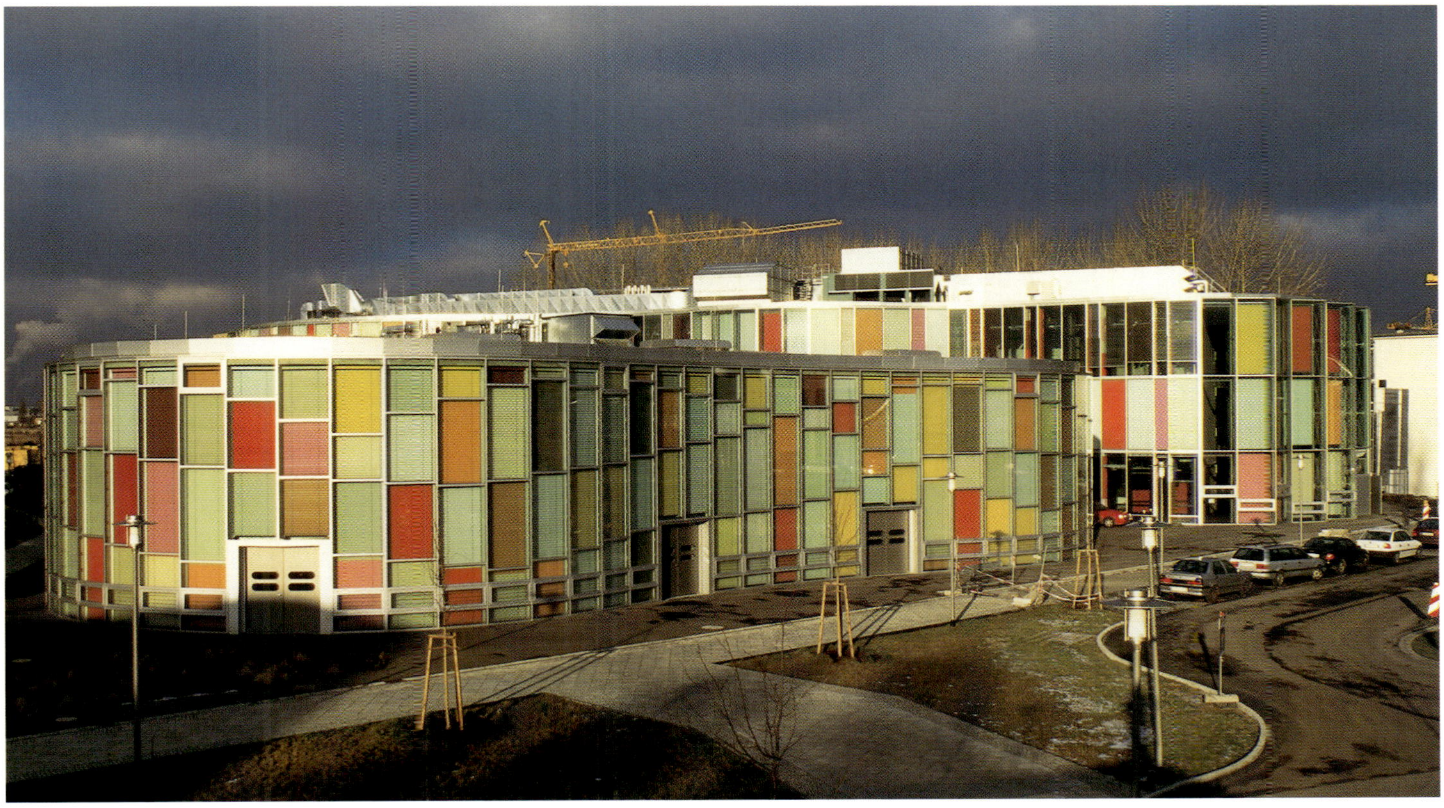

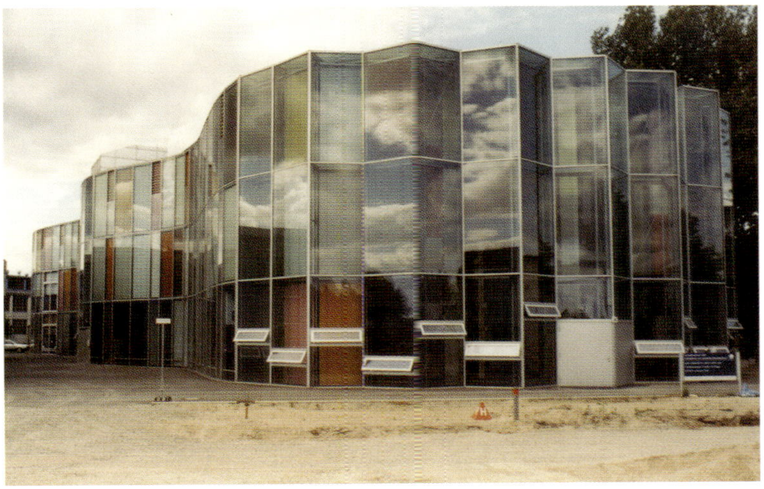

Innovationszentrum für Photonik
Sauerbruch Hutton, Berlin/London
1996–1997
Rudower Chaussee
Forschung
Scientific research
Centro de Investigación

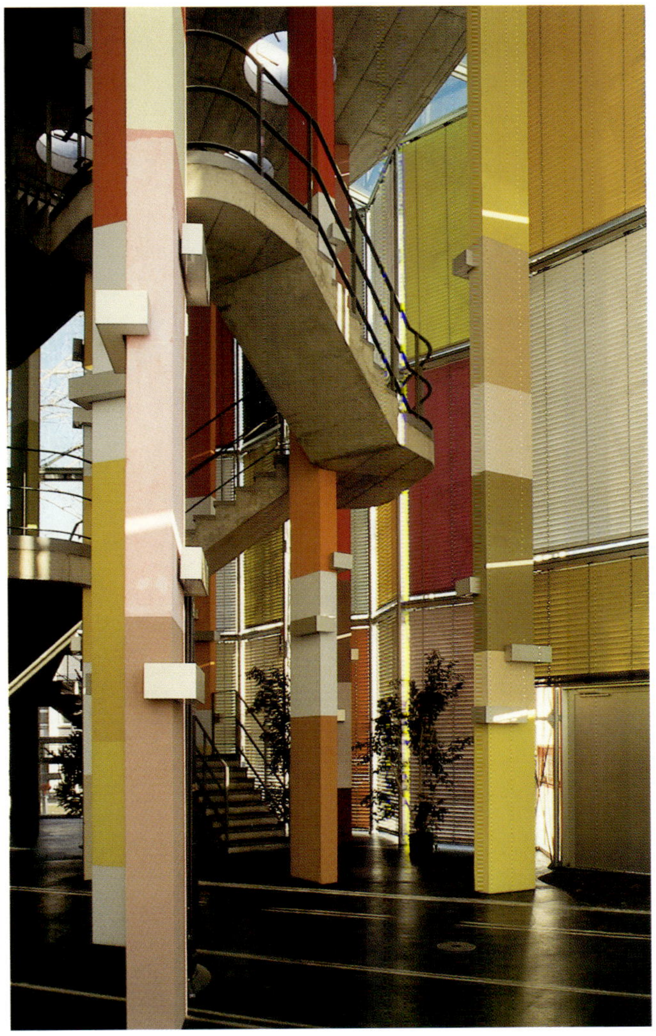

Kraftwerk Mitte
Power Station Mitte
Central Térmica de Mitte
Jochem Jourdan, Bernhard Müller, Frankfurt a.M.
1994–1996
Michaelkirchstraße · Köpenicker Straße

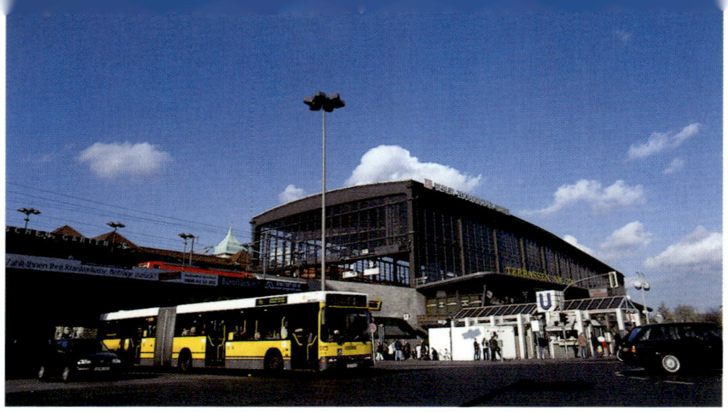

Bahnhof Zoologischer Garten
Fritz Hane
1934–1940

Bahnhof Spandau
gmp von Gerkan, Marg & Partner, Hamburg
Projektleitung: S. Zittlau-Kroos,
H. Nienhoff, K. Akay
1996–1998

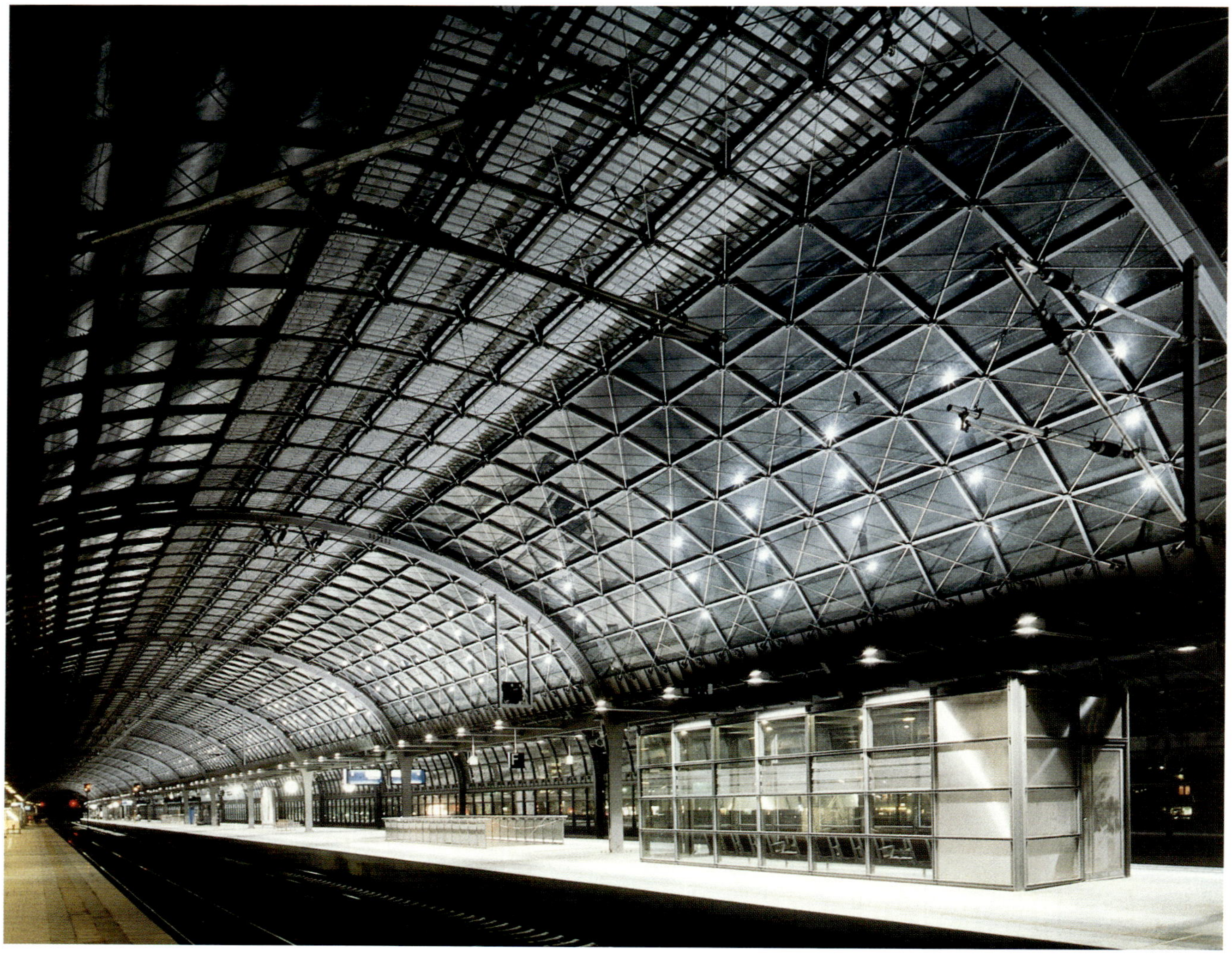

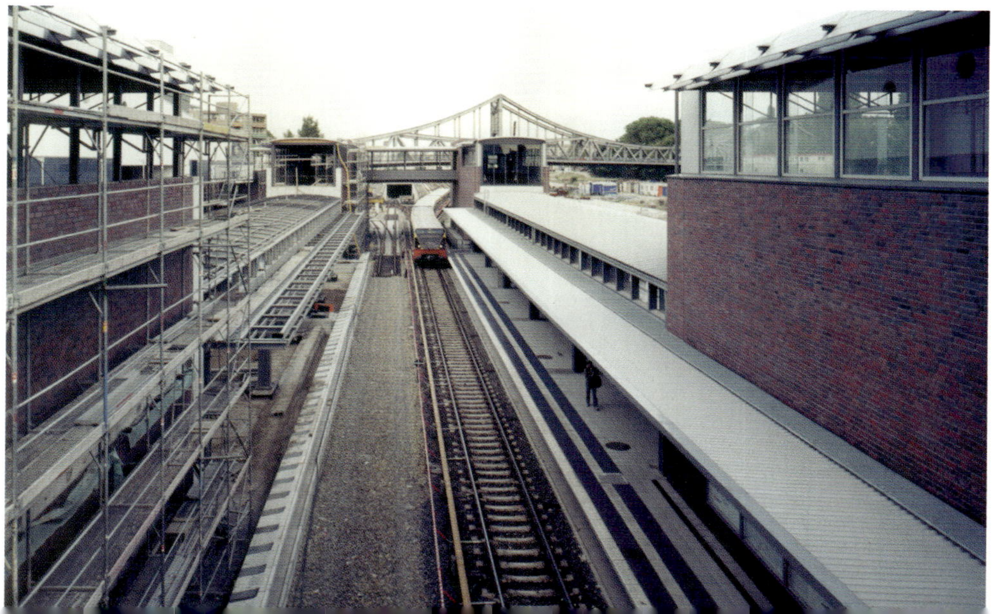

Bahnhof Berlin Gesundbrunnen
Axel Oestreich und
Ingrid Hentschel, Berlin
1996–1998

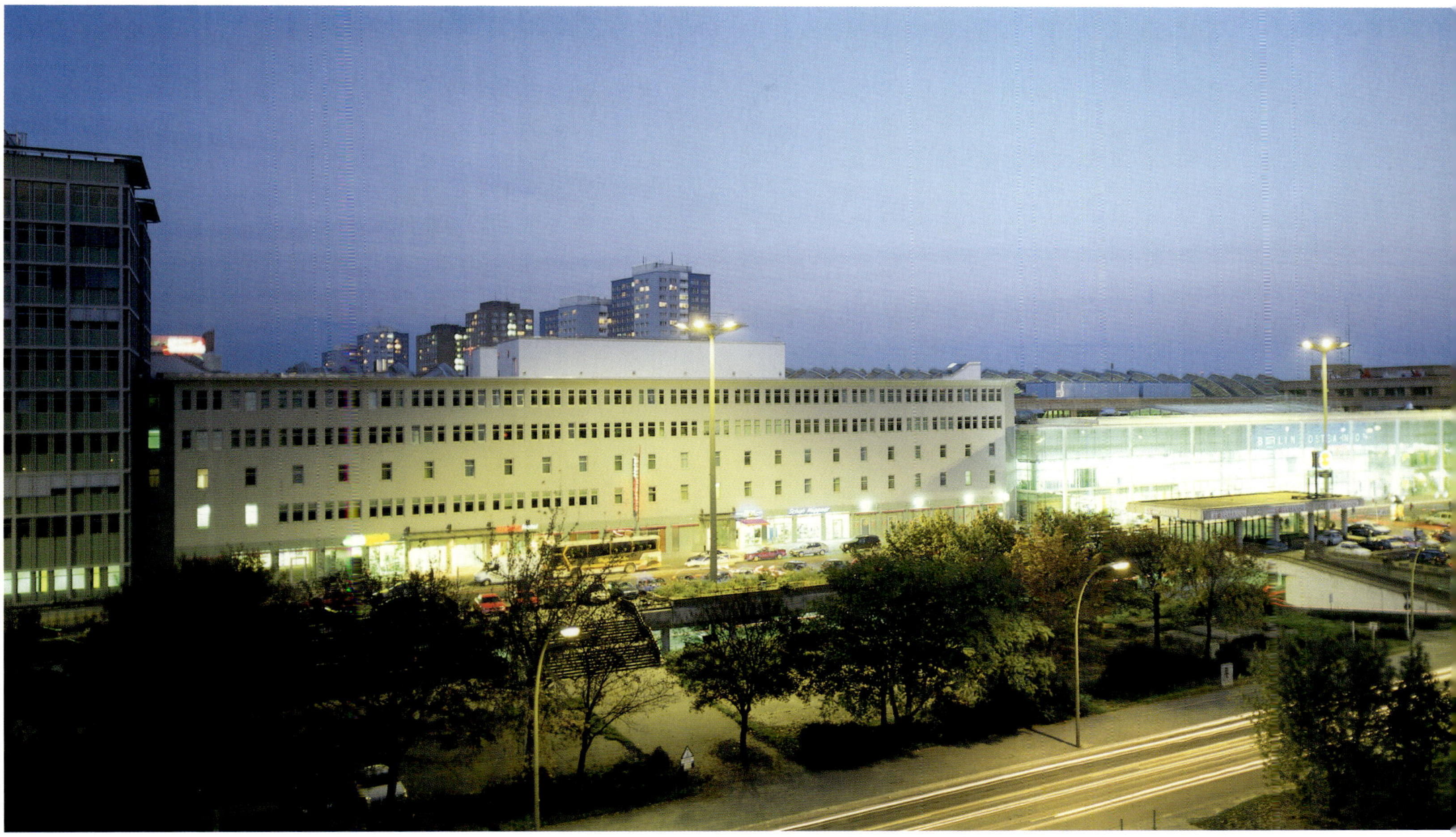

Ostbahnhof
Becker Gewers
Kühn & Kühn, Berlin
1998–2000

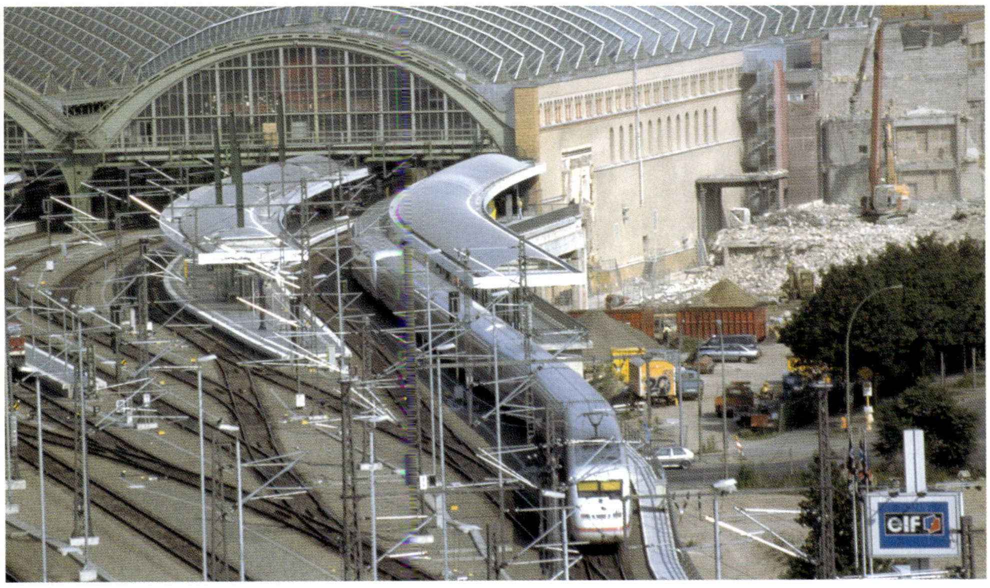

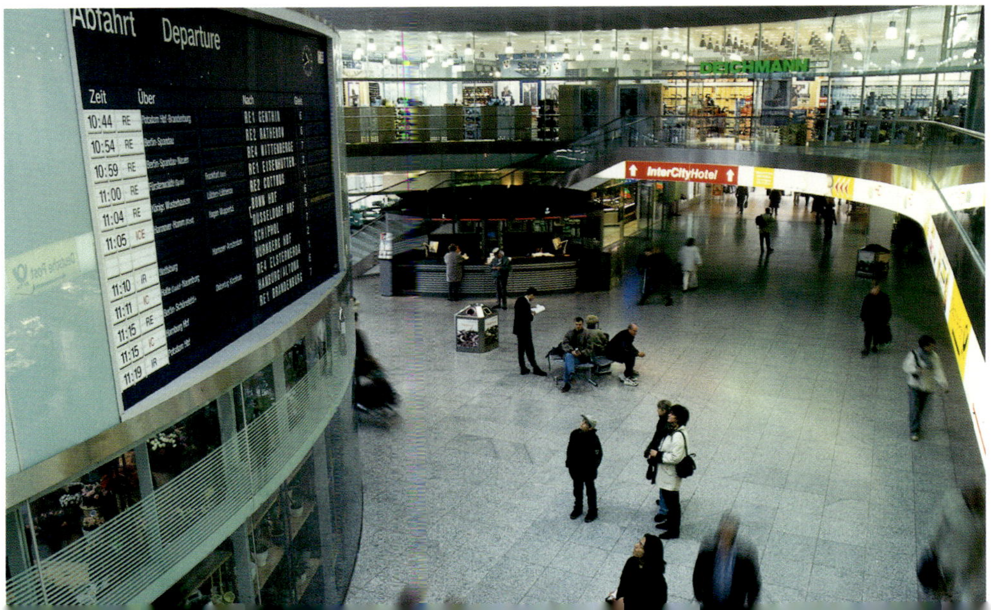

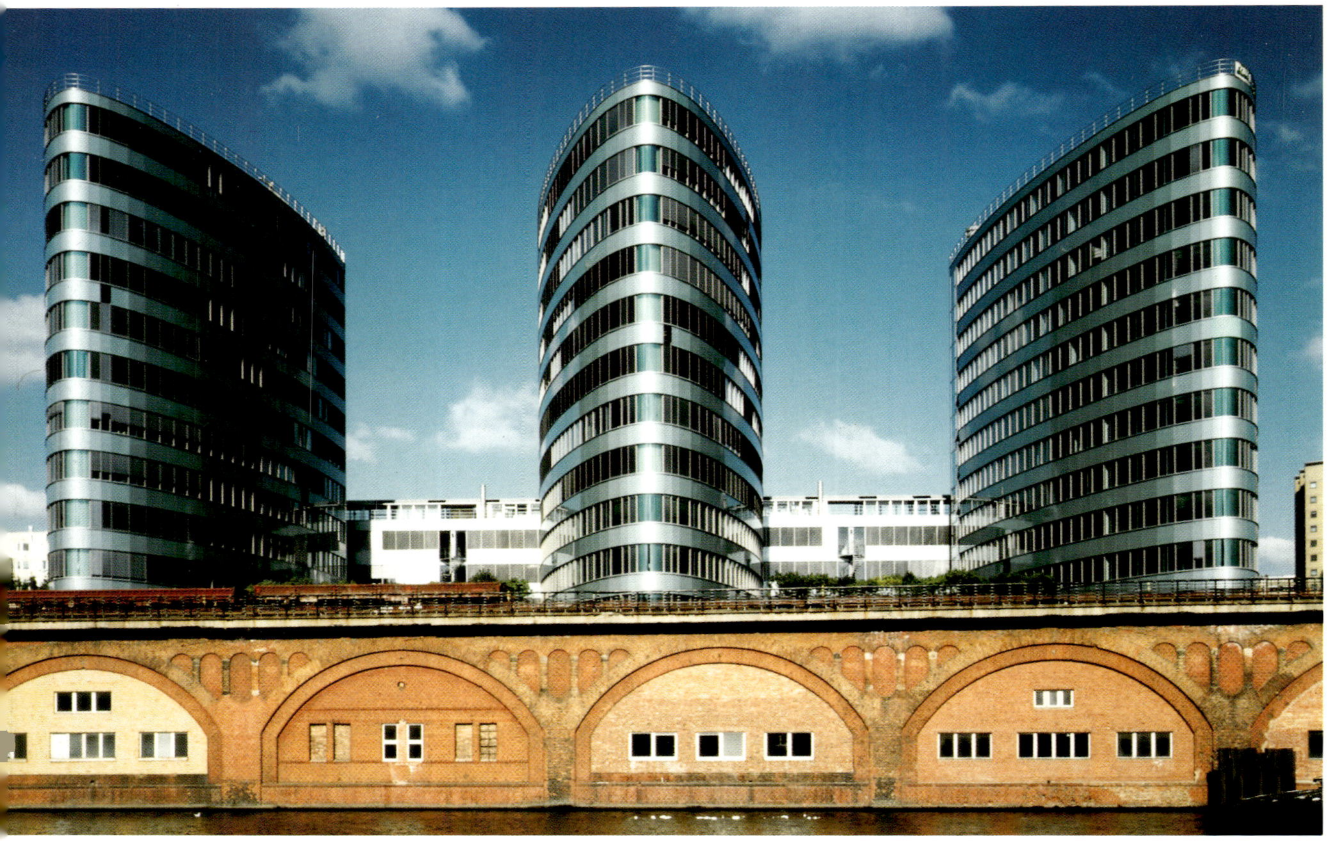

Büro- und Geschäftshaus Trias
Beringer & Wawrik, München
1993–1996
Holzmarktstraße
Büro, Gewerbe
Office, business
Oficina, comercio

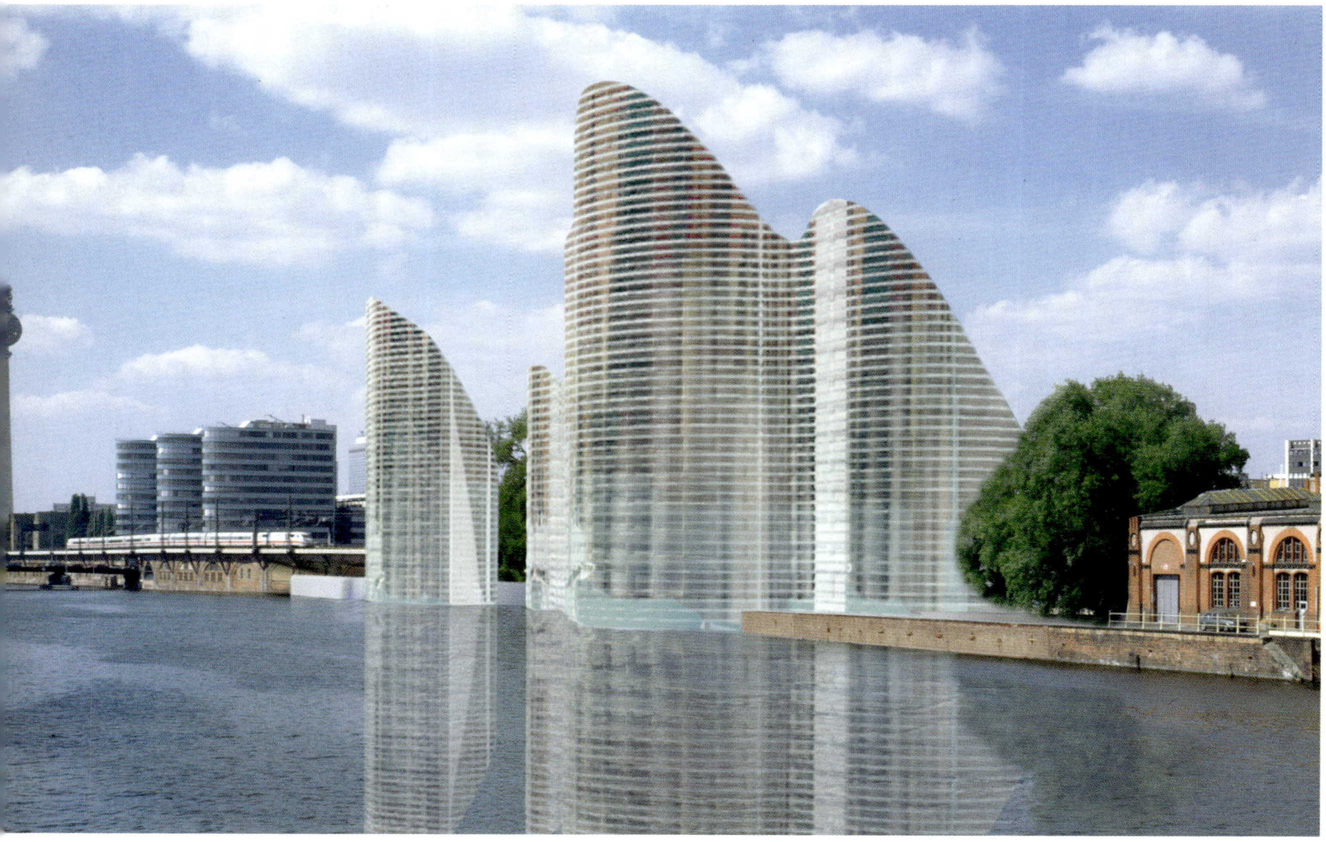

Spreesinus
Axel Schultes Architekten,
Frank, Schultes, Witt, Berlin
2002–2004
Holzmarktstraße
Büro, Gewerbe, Wohnen
Office, business, residence
Oficina, comercio, viviendas